CW00661318

A wonderful book, offering true [...]
real challenges in their own li[...]
humility is beautifully characteri[...]
faith and facts, providing a divine lens for others to see
through their circumstances to a living God who heals,
comforts and restores in the darkest of valleys.
Phil Shaw, European Director of Shake the Nations
Ministries

Written with humble honesty and compassionate
wisdom, Chris unfolds his personal story, giving the
reader hope and faith to face what seems impossible.
His real-life lessons learnt through pain, struggle and
adversity amid an ongoing terminal diagnosis show what
is possible when your life is rooted in a genuine
relationship with Jesus Christ. Through the highs and
lows of his day-to-day reality, Chris explains not only how
to survive but how to live beyond the limitations of an
illness that seeks to cut life short.
This story is not only for those facing
a life-threatening health issue, but for anyone who feels l
ike they are facing a mountain they can't climb.
Read on and discover what is possible for you.
Clive Urquhart, Senior Pastor of Kingdom Faith Church

Chris Kemshell knows God. This comes
through loud and clear as he tells his story with
disarming transparency and heart rendering honesty.
His love for God, people and his family cannot help but
move anyone who reads this book. His faith for
healing while anchored to reality and a commitment to
keep loving God no matter what is truly inspiring. Read
this book and you'll know the God he serves better.
Steve Campbell, Senior Pastor of C3 Church Cambridge

It is an honour to be asked to write an endorsement for this book, by my friend Chris Kemshell. I have known Chris for a number of years now and love the heart he has for God and for people. In this aptly named book, 'Cancer and the Cross', Chris takes you on a journey, a very real, honest journey about cancer, faith and victory. He talks candidly about the road he had to walk from diagnosis to victory. I know you will be inspired and your faith encouraged as you take time to read this very inspiring book. Thank you for letting us see and learn from your journey Chris.
Andy Elmes, Pastor of Family.Church

In this wonderfully authentic and inspiring book, Chris shares his life experience and the hard-won godly wisdom he has gleaned from his reflective journey with his Saviour, Jesus, through the consequences of Chris's life with the diagnosis of a terminal illness. Chris bravely allows us to witness what it means to live a life of practical worship and witness while holding, in faithful tension, his full acceptance of a challenging medical diagnosis, with his full-on relationship with a God Chris knows can and does heal. Quietly and surely, this book changes us and our perspective on the courageous, joyful life of a disciple's journey in adversity.
Dr Myles MacBean, National Director of Scripture Union England and Wales

As a family, we had to face the C-Word when our youngest son contracted a rare cancer at the back of his eye. Due to excellent medical care and the prayers of many people, he was healed of the disease over twenty years ago, for which we give glory to God. We have come to the same conclusions as Chris: Jesus is the healer, healing is filled with mystery, we can frame our world with our words and there is often a difference between facts and truth. Most importantly, the depths of the sacrificial death of Christ on the Cross meet the deepest pains, sorrows and sicknesses that humanity can face. This is an honest, authentic, faith-filled book that deserves wide readership.

Stuart Bell, Senior Pastor of Alive Church Lincoln

This book is an open and honest story of how faith shines brighter and better, even in the worst of circumstances. Chris courageously takes us on his journey, tackling head-on the brutal reality of facing a terminal diagnosis, while having a living faith in Jesus as his Healer. He pulls no punches, describing the low points, the hard places, the heartache and mental torment cancer and loss bring. But this is not a sad story! Chris tells us all, from his own experience, how to find very real solutions on the journey to healing. He navigates us through the low points to higher ground and shows us how to move from days of despair into living lives of hope.

Judith Butler, Senior Pastor of Kingdom Faith Church Taunton

I really cannot recommend this book highly enough! I literally couldn't put it down and read it in one sitting. A human story of great faith under extreme trial. A family's message of real hope under the fog of cancer, coupled with real practical biblical truth of how to walk through such a trying ordeal and be victorious. I've known Chris for more than twenty-five years; he is a tremendous brother and friend in the faith.

Oliver Evans, Pastor of Rock Church Bradford

CANCER
AND THE
CROSS

Thanks

My Mum and Dad: For bringing me up in the faith of Jesus. I will always be thankful for the grounding you gave me in faith and for the constant support and encouragement throughout my life.

My children—Jessica, Luke and Sophie: I can't thank you enough for inspiring me to dig deep. Each one of you has motivated me in your own way. Without your strength and encouragement, I would not be where I am today. From the bottom of my heart, I thank you, I am so proud of you and love you very much.

My wife, Lucy: For holding my hand throughout the ups and downs of this journey. For supporting me on hospital visits, for continuing to be there when I am at my lowest points. For being there when I have struggled and fallen short in my duties of a husband and dad. For praying with me and encouraging me to persevere when times are tough. For believing in me and being my biggest encourager; for championing me when I needed it the most. Lucy, I love you and thank God for you.

Matt Bird @PublishU: For leading me on the 'Writing my Book' course; for pushing me when I needed the motivation and didn't feel capable of completing the book. I would fully recommend Matt's course if you have a book in you that needs to be written.

Dedication

I would like to dedicate this book to the memory of Liz Munday and to all those who have gone before us and continue the struggle of living with a terminal illness. I have dedicated chapter seven of this book to Liz. It's called 'Faith Shines Through – Death is NOT Defeat'. Liz is enjoying life to the full as she lives in paradise with her Creator. She was a true friend and an incredible example to me of how to live a life with a terminal illness. Despite her struggle, she continued to live a life honouring to God. It was full of faith, full of joy, full of praise, dedicated to prayer and thanksgiving. It was a contagious lifestyle that drew people to God and into a deeper relationship with God. All while suffering was a tangible reality. Liz continued, as an elder, to help me lead God's people at Linton Free Church with hope and joy, embracing all that God has for us in His Word and through His Spirit. She is a remarkable woman, one of God's Generals. Thank you, Liz.

Contents

Foreword

I've known Chris for over a decade, but it feels like a lifetime! That sounds like an insult, but I mean it in the best possible sense. Sometimes you meet a person who brings a better version of yourself to the fore and this is Chris. Such a person is a rare gift. He is like a brother to me, who has stood by me in good times and bad. At times he seems to know me better than I know myself, or at the very least he inspires me to know myself better so that I may know God more deeply. If you take the time to read this book and capture a sense of the heart of the author, it will lead you to know more about the Author of life.

Chris may not imagine himself as a writer, but he has always been the most passionate and wonderful storyteller. The stories he shares have captured his heart and one could not fail to be drawn in by his enthusiasm. Now the story he has put to paper in this book. It captures his own story and is a beautiful thing, written to reflect the passion that all those who know him will recognise. The words of this book are true of the person I know in real life.

The vulnerability at the heart of Chris's story is true. From sharing with his family the diagnosis to being willing to put it into writing for others to see, it reflects so much of who he is. The phrase "he wears his heart on his sleeve" is perhaps overused, but ever so appropriate for Chris. And his heart belongs to Jesus and that shines through in this story.

Chris's hope for any reader is that we may discover hope when faced with a major setback. It reminds me of James words in his letter and what I was reminded of time and again as I read this book: "Consider it pure joy, my brothers and sisters, whenever you face trials of many kinds, because you know that the testing of your faith produces perseverance," (James 1:2-3). Chris mentions these verses being important to him and it resonated as I read. Here is a man who has been tested and within that he persevered and his faith matured. Chris inspires me and the way he has faced (and continues to face) life in all its variety has taught me so much about trials and testing, faith and friendship.

In sharing this story, Chris has not hidden his heart or the reality he faced, which at times did not go the way he, or others, expected. The story is all the richer for his honesty. It will relate to all readers as being real, in a world where we are rightly suspicious of much we read or watch. In this book, Chris shares what it is like to not only live with a cancer diagnosis but, much more than that, about how to face life's challenges through pregnancies, heartbreak, family struggles, bad times and good. It is an honest reflection on the rollercoaster that is life.

I highly recommend this book: it is not a fantasy reflection of what could have been, but the true story of a life lived fully committed to God.

Revd Russell Winfield, Dean of St Mellitus College

The front cover is a simple explanation of the message behind this book. Cancer in its darkness enters the light of our lives, bringing destruction, pain and fear. The Cross can be the light that enters that darkness and ultimately leads to hope, breakthrough and victory through Jesus.

Introduction

The thought of me being an author is something that I wouldn't imagine in my wildest dreams. I think even if they were honest, the people closest to me would say the same thing. I don't see myself as particularly academic. I am statemented for dyslexia, so writing doesn't 'float my boat' or is something I am particularly gifted at.

However, here I am—inspired to share my story. In this book, I share my experience of being diagnosed with terminal cancer. I share the immediate impact that has on my life and how my faith in God gives me a hope that my diagnosis is not the overshadowing identity in how I live the rest of my life. My hope and faith is in a living God who can intervene in life's circumstances that may seem impossible. I believe that the God I serve is my Healer and healing is possible today.

I look to personal stories and biblical truths that have shaped my understanding while not hiding from the realities of physical and emotional pain that cancer causes. This is a real journey that identifies with both the hope and suffering that you can face when living with such a diagnosis. I write about the inspiration that can be found through those who suffer while remaining full of faith and joy despite their suffering. And how cancer can be a catalyst for the power of God to be demonstrated in and through our lives.

The journey is ongoing and full of ups and downs. But the cancer doesn't need to define those who suffer. Victory is available and the life of acknowledging what Jesus has already accomplished on the Cross can lead to great breakthrough in our lives. This is not theory; it can be a genuine hope and a victorious way of living through the power of God and reality of His Word.

The front cover is a simple explanation of the message behind this book. Cancer in its darkness enters the light of our lives, bringing destruction, pain and fear. The Cross can be the light that enters that darkness and ultimately leads to hope, breakthrough and victory through Jesus. My hope is that as you read this book, you discover that there is hope for those who suffer major setbacks in their lives, however traumatic they may be. And that you ultimately encounter a living God that loves you with an everlasting love and can give you the tools for overcoming life's trials.

CANCER AND THE CROSS

The Cross has far more power and authority than cancer, or any other disease or ailment.
Therefore, if you were wondering? The C-Word stands for The Cross, not cancer.

Chapter One
The C-Word (early days)

I can remember the day clearly, but for some reason can't remember the exact date. I know it was sometime in the first week of September 2017. It was a normal working day. My wife, Lucy, was at work and my kids were at school.

The phone rang, it was a supply doctor from my local surgery. Very quickly I was told that I had carcinoid syndrome. I had experienced some severe pain, very randomly, over the last few years. After having some tests, my doctor was convinced that carcinoid syndrome was what I had, but this was not an official diagnosis. I was told that the hospital would be in contact with me very soon for scans but in the meantime, I should sit down and explore the NHS website about this disease.

Bang! This was like a sledgehammer! It hit me hard but didn't knock me out. I guess I was in shock. I felt quite numb. Although I had suffered some horrible pain, this possible diagnosis was totally unexpected. I quickly read that carcinoid syndrome (also known as NETS – neuroendocrine tumours) is a very rare type of terminal cancer, usually diagnosed in older people. I wanted to share my news with someone, but Lucy was at work, the children were at school and my family were not local. What do I do? How do I deal with this? Then I remembered I was due to visit a couple from church going through a difficult time. So, still in shock, I began to get on with my normal day-to-day routine.

The next few days were a bit of a blur. After speaking to Lucy, I think we were quite measured about this news. Maybe it's not as bad as it seems...of course, the doctor could be wrong! The information that we had read seemed very serious, but maybe it wasn't as serious as we first thought. We had just been out for a family meal before the children started a new term at school, but that evening I began to experience so much severe pain that Lucy called out the paramedics. This was not completely unusual as I had experienced severe pain on several occasions previously. I had been diagnosed as having irritable bowel syndrome, but this re-occurring pain did seem more sinister than that. Lucy and I will never forget that when the two paramedics were trying to give me pain relief, I shared with them the news that the doctor had given me previously. His face dropped and looked me straight in the eyes saying, "I am so sorry about this." I think at that moment we really knew how serious this was.

The following blog was written by my older brother; it gives his perspective on receiving this news:

My brother's blog (Paul Kemshell):

It is 8:29pm Friday 8th September (2017). Just got home, busy day! Work, kids, future plans, money, regrets, house sales, a head full of thoughts.

8:30pm: My younger brother calls, he tells me he has cancer and it has advanced and passed into a secondary area of his body. It seems, for just a moment, that the world has stopped spinning. What I considered important thirty seconds earlier suddenly has become totally irrelevant—my poor brother and what about his wife...his kids? The youngest has just started school this week. What about Mum and Dad? This seems so tough.

Then the world starts spinning again; I cannot even imagine how hard it must be for people that don't have faith in something bigger than what we can see.

Surprisingly, the overwhelming emotion is that of gratitude and thankfulness and a desire to make every moment count. There is so much in my life that I need to be grateful for, including my brother and his family.

8:42pm: Wished my brother good night and we prayed together.

People are precious and with a heavy heart, I think of times I have wronged people, where I was too abrasive or did not see the best in them, even put them down or let them down, or simply did not do what I said I would do. I wish I could turn back the clock and do things differently, but I can't. We can't! I think back to the schoolyard rhyme, "Sticks and stones will break my bones, but words will never harm me." But bones heal...

In a funny sort of way, this has been a special week. I drove down with my kids for a couple of hours to see my brother and we just hung out. We have spoken a couple of times each day on the phone just checking in on each other. Normally I could go a few weeks without talking to him. Why does it take a crisis to focus on what is important?

In very simple terms, cancer is a cell in our body that gets damaged and that starts to reproduce more and more damaged cells overpowering our healthy cells.

It's so easy to infect ourselves with virtual "cancer" of the heart, by holding on to hurt, unresolved bitterness and pain. We are not beholden to our past and we are not defined by our mistakes or the people that have hurt us. Life is simply too short and people are too precious not to live life, loving, with arms opened wide!

I am believing my God for a miracle, a miracle that gives me forty more years walking with my brother. But, if it's four weeks, four months or four years, I hope to remain grateful for what I have had, rather than what I might have lost. I guess, like me, you are not one of the one billion people on this amazing planet of ours that live on less than $1 per day. Let's not race to the bottom in self-pity but increase our love for those who have it worse than us. As part of your life seems to go up in flames, it might just be the smoke signal needed to attract heaven's blessings.

On Friday, 29th September 2017, a few weeks after I had been diagnosed with cancer and four days before my fortieth birthday, I was driving with my family to Yorkshire to see my parents.

I had not been driving long when God spoke to me. You may have no experience of God, never mind hearing God speaking to you. This wasn't an audible voice, but it was a strong conviction in my heart that couldn't be ignored. In recent years, I had found that God often speaks to me when I am about to drop off to sleep or when I am driving. When this happens, I have to either get up or pull over so that I can make notes—frustrating, but always worth it. On this occasion, I didn't need to pull over and make notes. We were worshipping, as we often do as a family in the car and listening to worship songs while singing along. As we did this, a voice in my head said, "Chris, I want you to write a book." I knew straight away that this was God speaking because He often speaks to me like this. And my experience is that He regularly asks me to do things that seem ridiculous: the idea of me writing a book was a ridiculous thought. God quickly then added, "The book will be called, 'Cancer and the Cross.'" Strangely enough, this seemed to be further confirmation that this was God speaking, as my first impression of the book title wasn't great.

I didn't have much time to process this before I was in hospital having a confirmed diagnosis of carcinoid syndrome requiring major bowel surgery to remove the tumours. The surgery was a huge success and they managed to remove the main tumour from my bowel. Obviously, this was great news—but it wasn't all great news. I was informed that the tumour wasn't caught in time and it had spread. I had several other tumours in the liver. Basically, there was nothing they could do. They made it clear, however, that although nothing could be done to remove the tumours, I could have an injection every four weeks to help prevent their growth. I was told that the tumours were slow-growing and would normally be found in people a lot older than me. It was also a rare type of cancer so there wasn't a massive amount of statistical information on life expectancy. All of this confirmed what I was originally told on the phone and what I discovered on the NHS website. This was the start of my journey with this terminal illness and all while having faith in a God that I believe to be my Healer.

In the early stages, one of the most challenging things to do was to speak to our children. We decided to do this early on in a park near to the hospital. This wasn't an easy decision as our children were young (nine, seven and five). But we wanted to be honest from the start and it was difficult to think of them hearing the news from anyone else. It was quite probable that they would hear from others because the nature of my job (a local church minister/pastor in a village community) meant that news travels. It would be difficult to hide this situation from others due to the amount of hospital visits that would be taking place. We wanted to face this together as a family. Our stance was clear: this wasn't a good situation with my health and we didn't know why it had happened. Being a family of faith, we wanted to be open with each other. Even more significantly, we wanted to be open with God. As a family, we pray, we talk to God and we listen to God. We also believe that with God nothing is impossible (Luke 1:37), so we wanted to let the children know that God is bigger than the health issue and is able to heal.

It is my personal faith that when Jesus, the Son of God, suffered, died on a Cross and rose from death over two thousand years ago, He did it for everyone—no one is excluded. One of the benefits from this act of God is that healing can be accessed because of what Jesus accomplished on the cross.

The Cross has far more power and authority than cancer, or any other disease or ailment. Therefore, if you were wondering? The C-Word stands for The Cross, not cancer.

This is not easy, but I made a decision early on that I would shower myself with the positive promises and declarations that the Bible has for me. These are spiritualtruths that I feel can be a reality if I activate them in my life.

Chapter Two

Choosing Your Identity

I know I have been diagnosed with a rare type of terminal cancer. It is a reality in my life. But my faith tells me that my God is the Healer and I believe that God can heal me. As crazy as it sounds, I also believe God has already healed me. That assertion needs unpacking (which I will aim to do throughout this book), but it stems from what Jesus has already accomplished on the Cross. I can remember the look in the doctor's eyes when I have told them, "God can heal me from this." Their look is not necessarily one of affirmation or agreement but rather a look of sympathy or confusion.

My life has been grounded around a Christian belief. I know that I am accepted and loved by a God who sent His Son to die for me. I have experienced many highs and lows as well as great loss and great victory. (Again, we will look at this in greater detail throughout this book.) I have prayed many times and not seen the answers that I was expecting. But I have also seen God miraculously transform situations and at times, answer prayers in ways that I can only explain as being supernatural. Don't write me off at this point for being a lunatic! Throughout this book I will take you on my personal journey of living with a terminal diagnosis while also looking at biblical truths and personal experience of why this diagnosis is not something by which I want to be identified.

I've been a minister in the church for ten years; I've been actively involved in church leadership for many years; I've been twice to Bible college and I've lived a life of faith for nearly forty years (I write this in 2023, six years after my diagnosis). Nevertheless, I can happily hold my hands up in the air and tell you I don't have full understanding on healing. I struggle with people who suggest that they do have a full understanding. I do have some knowledge on this topic; I do have some knowledge on what the Bible teaches on this subject; and I also have some valuable experience on this topic. What I can say is that there is a mystery to the topic of healing and I do not claim to have full understanding about it.

I believe in the Bible teachings of Jesus healing the sick, doing miraculous signs and even raising the dead. I believe in an all-powerful God who has demonstrated His power throughout the teachings in the Bible. I have also seen this power being released in people's lives today (I will share some of those stories later in this book). I have prayed with sick people and they have recovered; I have seen people supernaturally recover from addictions; I have even seen limbs grow as I was praying. All these experiences are ones that cannot be taken from me and I know them to be true. These experiences obviously help me in terms of faith and in knowing that there is a God who is able to heal and has indeed healed.

I can't share these experiences, however, without sharing the other side. I have also prayed for healing and not seen it take place. I have been with people of incredible faith, but they didn't receive their healing in the way they were expecting or hoping. I have seen some people recover who didn't seem to have faith, while others did not recover despite having seemingly incredible faith. I think it's OK if we sometimes don't understand or know why. I know that there is a God who is able to heal, who has power and continues to demonstrate that power throughout people's lives today.

I believe faith has a major part of this process but, to reiterate, I don't mind admitting that I don't have all the answers.

So, let's get to the purpose of this chapter. In my position, I had the dilemma of receiving the diagnosis, continuing to take medications and advice from my doctors, while knowing and totally believing that my best friend, Jesus, is my Healer. Maybe you can relate to this; maybe you know someone in this kind of position. I have met many people of faith over the years who might find themselves in a similar position to this. They change their view on healing due to receiving or not receiving what they expected in prayer. I understand that there can be a hesitance to believe, due to the fear of being disappointed in case God doesn't heal. But my experience and understanding of the Bible means I simply can't ignore my belief that Jesus is my Healer today, despite my circumstances.

This dilemma leaves me with a choice of my identity. Do I fully embrace the diagnosis in the sense that it becomes my identity? Or do I fully embrace my faith and belief that my God is my Healer? Or maybe there is a middle ground?

Let me try and give an example of what I mean. We all have thoughts. I wouldn't say that I have audible voices going on in my head, but I think things. One day, I was walking home after I had dropped the children off at school. There were a number of things to do that day, but it was good weather and I was happy about the day ahead. As I walked past the local pub in our village, I heard, "I wonder who will take Luke for his first pint?"

Luke is my twelve-year-old son who is clearly not ready for his first pint, but this was a thought about the future. This hit me hard. It felt like it came out of nowhere. I had never even thought of taking Luke for his first pint. What was this about? This is often how I feel God speaks to me but this time, it was not God. This seemed such a cruel and unnecessary thing to hear or think. I am hoping you be able to relate to this by imagining this kind of situation happening.

What has this story got to do with what I am writing about? It shows my response to what was going to influence my day. I had a choice: I could, understandably, get quite depressed about this thought and dwell on it. To be honest, I am not too concerned about taking my son for his first pint, but I want to be around when it happens. I want to see my children grow and see them get married; I want to grow old with my wife and I want to meet my grandchildren. At that moment, I had a choice. Was my choice to focus on the negative thought: diagnosis, who else will take Luke for a pint and how long do I have? Or should I think more positively? It just so happened that as I walked past the pub and was coming to terms with what had just occurred, I received a text message with this Bible verse:

"May the God of hope fill you with all joy and peace as you trust Him, so that you may overflow with hope by the power of the Holy Spirit" (Romans 15:13).

As I read it, I turned around looking for the person, convinced that they had either heard this voice or knew exactly what was going on. Of course, they were not there, but their text message helped me make a good choice. So, I began to thank God for His joy and peace in my life. Doing that transformed my thinking and mentality. You see, at that moment I believe I had two realities going on: one was the cancer and the negative situation; the other was the truth that God is with me and He has given me peace and joy, which is what I believe is a truth of Scripture. It doesn't always feel like a truth but when I activate that truth in my life it feels like truth. Every day, I get several of these examples. Some may not be as extreme as this, but this is a continuing journey.

The Bible also tells us in the second part of 2 Corinthians 10:5 that we are to "take captive every thought to make it obedient to Christ".

Not every thought is in agreement with what the Bible says about our life. My journey so far has taught me that this is a great discipline that people of faith have to practice. Actually, this is not only true for people of faith. Anyone can focus on the positives and practice being positive. Unfortunately, I have come across many people who are generally negative about situations. The first thing that they will say will be a negative word or a negative expression, maybe saying things such as: "This always happens to me." "Life is so unfair!" Or "Other people don't have my problems." They seem to cultivate that kind of mentality. Rarely would they speak in a positive manner or even smile. Of course, many people go through horrible life experiences and have reason to be down. I don't want to give people a hard time because of that. But I think there is something about choosing our identity, which is what this chapter is about.

This is not easy, but I made a decision early on that I would shower myself with the positive promises and declarations that the Bible has for me. These are spiritual truths that I feel can be a reality if I activate them in my life. Throughout this book, we will look at different ways in which I have learnt to do this. But this involves taking every thought captive and it involves making a choice when I wake up to declare things such as, "Today, I am going to 'Give thanks to God! Because He gives us the victory through our Lord Jesus Christ'" (1 Corinthians 15:57). Or "Today I am going to 'Be strong in the Lord and in His mighty power'" (Ephesians 6:10). I will try to do this at the start of and throughout the day. And I will try to do this regardless of how I am feeling. When I start to feel low and feeling sorry for myself, this is when speaking these words out loud are most effective. That is my experience. I don't think this is a case of me denying my personal experience or not recognising it. But I think this is placing God's Word and, what God says on an issue, right into the centre of my situation.

My experience is that when you get a diagnosis you can be overloaded with thoughts, information, medication, appointments, letters, etc. The danger for me is that I become so overloaded and consumed by the diagnosis, medical situation or whatever, that it becomes my identity. It becomes what I think about, what I talk about, who I am. I don't want this to happen. This doesn't mean that I ignore the information, the doctors, medication, appointments, letters, etc., but I balance them out with what the Bible says about me.

As a child of God, I believe the Bible says a lot about me. I try and listen to positive uplifting music, mostly Christian worship, although it doesn't have to be exclusively worship. For instance, I was having a tough day recently and a song from twenty years ago came to mind. It was D:Ream's 'Things Can Only Get Better' so I blasted it out and soon I had a spring in my step and was feeling far more positive about my situation. I try and put myself around positive people that I know will speak positively to encourage me. There are different things we can decide to do that will help or hinder our situation.

Conversely, as a teenager, I can remember thinking I was in love with a certain girl. I found out that the feeling wasn't mutual. In that situation I made the choice to listen to love songs that at the time seemed to break me. I laugh to myself as I write this, but all that particular music did was help me go deeper into feeling sorry for myself and feeling increasingly depressed about the situation.

Every day, we have choices that determine where we are heading. I hate being labelled a cancer patient. It's crazy but it does have one advantage in that if you want to see a doctor, it seems far more likely you'll see someone quickly if you have a cancer diagnosis. But I certainly don't like the label. Maybe writing a book isn't the most helpful thing I can do to get rid of that label. My personal identity is not in what has been medically diagnosed over my life. Rather, my identity is what God says about me. Consequently, I use promises from the Bible to help me remain rooted in those promises, identifying myself with what God says about me rather than what the world says or how I sometimes feel. What I find is that when I do this, it uplifts my spirit and I begin to feel increasingly positive about my situation and how I identify myself. Here are five examples of how I do this using biblical promises...

Promise from the Bible

"For the Spirit God gave us does not make us timid, but gives us power, love and self-discipline" (2 Timothy 1:7).

Personalised Declaration

I don't need to be fearful of anything that is happening in my life— because God has given me power, love and self-discipline to overcome any fear.

Promise from the Bible

"This was to fulfil what was spoken through the prophet Isaiah: 'He took up our infirmities and bore our diseases'" (Matthew 8:17 NIV).

Personalised declaration

No matter what I feel like today, I am choosing to believe what the Bible tells me. That Jesus Himself took up my sickness and disease on the Cross. Help me today to live in this truth.

Promise from the Bible

"Cast all your anxiety on Him because He cares for you" (1 Peter 5:7 NIV).

Personalised declaration

I am amazed that you care for me personally, God, so much so that You want me to throw all my anxiety in Your direction. I do not need to be anxious about anything that is troubling me today.

Promise from the Bible

"Trust in the LORD with all your heart and lean not on your own understanding; in all your ways submit to Him and He will make your paths straight" (Proverbs 3:5-6).

Personalised declaration

In all I do today I will put my trust in You, God. I will look to You for guidance in all areas of my life, not trusting in my own situations, circumstances or limited understanding. Thank You for Your direction in my life, God.

Promise from the Bible

"Now to Him who is able to do immeasurably more than all we ask or imagine, according to His power that is at work within us" (Ephesians 3:20 NIV).

Personalised declaration

God, I am amazed by the thought of your power working through me today. Help me, God, make this my identity today that in whatever I do, You can use me and work through me. Thank You that Your plans for me are bigger than I can imagine. I am living for You today and I make myself available for You to use me.

Never once did I feel discouraged, fearful, anxious or down after worshipping. It always activated hope, faith, joy, expectancy and peace, even in the middle of the trial.

Chapter Three
Experiences That Shaped My Understanding

Often in life it is our experiences that shape our understanding and values that we place in our lives. This is the case whether we are looking through a faith lens or not. I have had many experiences that have influenced my perspective on where I am today. In this chapter, I am sharing three personal stories that have had a significant impact on shaping how I understand faith and how the God that I trust heals today.

Toby Jack

Lucy and I were married in March 2003. Life was fantastic, we were fresh out of Bible college, full of faith and ready to start married life together. We moved to Bradford, where we would begin the first chapter of our married life together. Lucy was teaching and I was working for a church running a centre that worked mainly with young offenders. It was always our desire to start a family but like many people, we found that this wasn't straight forward. In short, we were offered IVF in 2006. We were all set to start this process when, amazingly, Lucy fell pregnant.

We were so happy and began to make plans for the future. We had recently bought a house and began to decorate the nursery. Everything seemed to be wonderful: family, friendships, church life and work were all good. We were so thankful. I loved Lucy being pregnant and would read up on how the pregnancy was going so I could send weekly updates to family and friends; I signed off these updates "Daddy Cool".

I want to share with you some of what I wrote on the 30 August 2006: "Hi guys, great news. We are back from a fantastic holiday in London and Devon. Baby has been incredibly active over the last few weeks including two sessions in the nice and cold southern sea.

"Baby is about twenty-six cm and weighs about 1.25kg. Baby Cool is growing and developing at top speed. Baby's brain is growing so quickly that the soft skull bones are being pressed outwards and his/her head is now in proportion to the rest of his/her body. Baby's brain now looks wrinkled as it gets faster and more powerful, building up connections between nerves and cells. Baby's brain can now control his/her breathing and body temperature. Baby's eyes can now move in their sockets and he/she is becoming more sensitive to light, sound, taste and smell.

"I will end with this, it's flipping amazing, through the wall of the uterus baby can now tell the difference between sunlight and artificial light. God is awesome. Be blessed, Daddy Cool."

Sharing this highlighted the excitement and reality of the situation we were in. I had been sending these emails from the start of the pregnancy, so we were fully aware of how the baby's progress was. It was such an amazing time, but we didn't realise what was round the corner.

Two days after this email was sent, Toby Jack was stillborn on the 1 September, 2006. We were totally heartbroken that the miracle of Toby would then be taken away from us. Even in the moments that Toby was born, I was desperately praying for a miracle even though we already knew what had happened. A week after Toby was stillborn, I wrote my final "Daddy Cool" email, here is a portion of it:

"Dear friends, I am sure most of you will have heard, but for those who haven't I am emailing you with some very sad news. On the 1 September at 9:54am Lucy gave birth to our precious son who was stillborn. Toby Jack weighed 3lb 2oz and was beautiful.

"As you can imagine, we are devastated by this and appreciate your love and prayers at this time. From the moment Lucy and I discovered Lucy was pregnant, Toby Jack became so special and was loved so much by Mummy and Daddy.

"Even though Lucy and I are heartbroken at this time we want to thank God for the time and wonderful memories we have of Toby Jack's short life. We know that Toby has gone to be with his Creator and that gives us great joy amongst our grief. Toby means "God is good" and Jack means "Jehovah has favoured" or "God is gracious". These are very special meanings for a very special boy and Toby would have loved us to reflect on these meanings as a result of his life. God bless and love from Mummy and Daddy Cool."

It has been difficult to share this and the memories are still very real, nearly eighteen years on. In simple terms, this was a situation where we were desperately believing for a healing to take place. It didn't happen in the way I was planning it out in my head. Why? The truth is I don't know. Did this experience rock me? Yes, it did. Did this experience cause incredible pain and give us unanswered questions? Yes, of course. One thing this experience didn't do was uproot my faith. I think the main reason was that my faith was built on firm foundations that were not dependant on what God did for me.

In concluding this first story, I have realised that to not have full understanding is a great place to be. Simply because we don't require faith if we have full knowledge and understanding. Being able to realise that we may not fully understand or comprehend the things of God places us in a position where we need to trust. We can fully trust God and His ways, but we won't always understand God's purpose and ways. After all, faith is having confidence in something/someone without always knowing the outcome.

Sophie Jane

Fast forward to July 2013. God has been so good to us since we lost Toby Jack. We now have two children, Jessica Faith (aged four) and Luke Christopher (aged two). Lucy is also twenty-five weeks pregnant. We have moved from Bradford to Cambridge. Lucy is loving being a full-time mum and I have obtained a degree in theology and am about to be ordained as minister of Linton Free Church, Cambridgeshire. When I say about to be ordained, I am taking you back to the 10 July, 2013, which was a normal day and was three days before I was ordained.

We were getting ready for family coming to visit for the ordination. But something didn't quite feel right with the pregnancy and experience told us that we should go to the hospital. With Jessica and Luke sorted, we headed into hospital. In hospital, there was concern but Lucy very quickly sensed God reassuring her that this would not be the same experience as it was with Toby. We were trusting God, but things were moving very quickly. I don't know if it was particularly quiet in hospital that day, but it seemed like everyone was in the room to witness the unexpected birth of Sophie Jane. It was clearly a good decision to head into hospital.

Very quickly, but with much trauma, Sophie was born at twenty-five weeks, four weeks before Toby was born. She was taken from us and only weighed 1.4lbs. When we eventually saw Sophie, she was brought to us in an incubator, but we couldn't touch her as she was very vulnerable. She was no bigger than my small hand. Her skin was so thin that you could see through it. Sophie was fighting for her life and we were just about to embark on another journey that required faith and trust in God. This all happened so quickly and, as I write, I can remember holding Lucy's hand while she was amazingly reassuring me of what God had earlier reassured her about. This was not going to end in the way it did for Toby. What an amazing thing for her to focus on in the middle of what was another trial.

There is so much that can be said about this experience, but Sophie was to stay in hospital for three months. This journey wasn't easy at all. We were told very regularly not to get carried away and even say our goodbyes to Sophie before she was taken off for further treatment at various times. This went on for some time, but we never said goodbye to Sophie—we were fighting with her. It wasn't easy but every time we saw her and at different times throughout the days ahead, we would thank God for our healthy little girl. This really wasn't easy, especially when we could see how fragile and weak she was. Thankfully, we were given accommodation in the hospital grounds so one of us could be there day and night while the other looked after Jessica and Luke at home. Days went into weeks and eventually we were able to hold Sophie. We will never forget those first cuddles.

There were plenty of ups and downs and lots of advice for us not to get carried away, but there was something about Sophie that helped us to believe big. Although she was so small and fragile, she had a big heart and was helped by stimulation through a caffeine drip. The word that God spoke to Lucy about this being a different situation to Toby was like a launchpad for us to take hold of and claim over little Sophie. Proverbs 18:21 says, "The tongue has the power of life and death." This was a reality for us in our situation. We were continuously speaking life and thanking God for life over our daughter.

You could sense the concern from people around us as we were being so positive in this situation. It was a genuine concern that we were certainly not through the woods and if things were going to turn, we would have a greater fall from how positive we were being. This was not a stress-free journey where simple positivity transformed the situation. For one, it was clear that the medical expertise of the specialist doctors and the ongoing treatment of the dedicated nurses were absolutely essential for Sophie's progress. And there were certain times where doubts and fears would trickle in and make the journey less smooth. But the positivity and holding onto the word that God had given us gave us hope. The more we spoke and declared that affirming word it strengthened the hope that we had and it became increasingly secure in our hearts, minds and lives.

There is a verse in Hebrews 6:19 which says, "We have this hope as an anchor for the soul, firm and secure." Even though our hope was firm and secure, like an anchor, it didn't mean that it was an easy ride. On the occasions when I have been to theme parks on dramatic roller coasters, I have felt confident in the structure of the ride, otherwise I wouldn't get on. But that doesn't mean that the ride is always peaceful and stress free. As we heard the word for Sophie that we believed to be from God, we spoke it daily. As we spoke that word it did something to our faith. Romans 10:17 puts it this way: "Faith comes from hearing the message and the message is heard through the word about Christ." Our faith was ready for the battle.

At one point in the journey, I took a photo of my wedding ring over Sophie's hand, the ring was larger than her hand. Sophie's hand would easily go through my ring and the ring would go up her arm and over her shoulder. This is a constant image I have of how small Sophie really was.

Again, I fast forward. I am writing this today on Sophie's tenth birthday. Sophie stayed in hospital for nearly three months. She was able to come home with feeding tubes just before her original due date. Sophie has incredibly gone from strength to strength, literally smashing barriers out of the way. There is no sign of any prematurity and she is a strong, healthy, full-of-joy ten-year-old. It is truly amazing how Sophie's life has turned out and we believe that we have seen God's healing hand on her life. There is no doubt that God has used the skills of doctors to bring about Sophie's healing, but I certainly wouldn't disregard God's supernatural intervention on her life.

Mum

The final story I am looking at in this chapter involves my mum, Denise Kemshell. On the morning of Monday 30 November, 2015, I had just taken an assembly at the local junior school when I got a call from my Dad saying that my Mum had been taken into hospital with an earache.

There was some obvious concern, but it didn't seem to be too serious when I received the initial call. But something didn't sit right and I felt I needed to take the three-and-a-half-hour journey up to Yorkshire from Cambridge to see my Mum. That was the right call as halfway into the journey I got the message that this was far more serious than first thought. I can remember this journey well: it was horrible; I didn't know really what was happening, but I had the sense that this was not good at all.

It turned out that my mum had had a CT scan that showed an infection in the ear that had spread to her brain. She was being transferred from one hospital to another so that she could have neurosurgery. Mum had dramatically deteriorated throughout the day and when I arrived, she was waiting for brain surgery. My brother was flying home early from work in Australia. Mum's first operation was to remove the infected part of the brain and drain the pus and, secondly, to drain the infected ear. After the four-hour operation we were told the chance of survival was fifty-fifty.

Another scan took place that showed that a further three-hour operation was needed. We were then told that there was a good chance of mum making a full recovery. This was an intense few days of the unknown but as a family, we rallied and prayed together, reading from the Bible to Mum and trying to be positive. It took Mum several days to come round from the sedation and effects of the infection. At first, she could only open her eyes and there was a vacant expression.

I had headed back to Cambridge to see my family on 11 December. As I was taking the exit of the motorway to my home, I pulled over to answer a call from my Dad. He had been told that the brain stem may be permanently damaged and that there could be no further progress from what we were getting: open eyes but no movement. I was broken by this news and was convinced that as I read Scripture to Mum in hospital, I received the faintest of hand squeezes from my mum. The news was that there had to be significant improvement in the next forty-eight hours, or they would recommend turning off all her machines that were keeping her alive.

After a short stop at home, I needed to head back to Yorkshire. Surely, this wasn't the end for Mum, I certainly wasn't ready to lose her. Dad was quite adamant that this was not her time, so prayer and fasting became increasingly pressing. Quite miraculously, within an hour of this news, mum did begin to squeeze hands. The next morning the "do not resuscitate" was rescinded. Mum was officially worth saving. On December 14th, the breathing tube was taken out and mum began to talk.

As with all these stories there is plenty of fast forwarding. Today, in 2023, Mum is at home. She can walk, she is fully aware and has some brain damage but has good functional capacity. Granted, Mum has not made a complete recovery in terms of mobility but there is no doubt that God has done a supernatural healing in her body.

I said at the start of this chapter that these three stories that I have shared have had a significant impact on shaping how I understand faith and how the God that I trust heals today. These stories don't give me full understanding or structures that can guarantee a format for God's healing to take place in situations for today. They do give me hope, however and they give me faith that with God nothing is impossible.

They also talk to me about perspective and how we view the personal trials that we all face at different seasons in our lives. In this life I will never fully understand why Toby Jack was taken from us; but one thing I realise is that if we hadn't gone through the experience, we would never have rushed to hospital in 2013 when Lucy was pregnant with Sophie. It is an incredible thought that in losing Toby, we gained Sophie. There is no doubt that from a medical perspective we would have lost Sophie if we didn't go to hospital on 10th July 2013.

The significance of worship

In concluding this chapter, there is something that we were able to do throughout all three of these experiences that helped us keep our focus on God rather than the circumstances we faced. We continued to worship God whatever situation we were in. This is by no means an in-depth breakdown of what worship is but, hopefully, this will give practical insight about how worship can impact our day-to-day lives in genuine ways. For me, worship is communicating to God the praise and honour of which He is worthy, not only with our lips but through our lifestyle. What I am focusing on is worship with our lips, expressing our love to God through singing.

The Bible teaches us in Colossians 3:16: "Let the message of Christ dwell among you richly as you teach and admonish one another with all wisdom through psalms, hymns and songs from the Spirit, singing to God with gratitude in your hearts."

My experience has been that when I express my love for God through singing, then whatever I feel like, it does something positive inside of me. It is as though I am choosing to put my dependence on God, rather than the life situation I face. It enables the Word of Christ to become increasingly activated within my life. This was especially the case during the fight of seeing Sophie grow and gain strength in her early days. Worshipping God was a key factor in not only giving us strength but increasing our faith for God to be a reality in our situation.

At the time, the situation with Sophie looked bleak and we were told it was indeed bleak. If our focus remained on the condition that Sophie was in, there is no doubt that our hope would have diminished. The worship enabled us to take our eyes off the circumstances and focus on God. Simply, we would continue to worship God through song despite how we felt at the time. There were times when we had to dig deep to physically do this but what we found was that when we did, it had an incredible effect on our mentality and well-being. This became a huge priority for us in this season of our lives; we would literally worship God at any given opportunity.

I can remember softly singing over the incubator and when I was out walking. Our car was like a temple of worship as we drove in and out of hospital. Never once did I feel discouraged, fearful, anxious or down after worshipping. It always activated hope, faith, joy, expectancy and peace, even in the middle of the trial. There were additional advantages to this, too: it brought Lucy and I together in a situation where, sadly, many distance themselves from each other. The conscious decision that Lucy and I made to be relentless in worship when Sophie was fighting for her life was one of our great decisions. Again, this wasn't always easy, but it made a significant difference to how we viewed the situation and it even changed how we felt. It created a confidence that God would restore Sophie; the hope was tangible. It also created a joy in our hearts that only God could give in the circumstance that we were facing.

Even after the loss of Toby, we would pick ourselves up and give God praise. This was not always easy, but I found that this would prevent feelings of rejection from God and allowed me to refocus and improve my faith outlook. It felt like I was having victory for Toby when I picked myself up and praised God instead of blaming Him.

I have found that worshipping God is like medicine for the body. Sometimes, I must take medicine when I don't feel like it, but I know it's good for me. Being totally honest, I don't always feel like worshipping God; sometimes I am tired, beaten up by my circumstances and not in the mood. But that quickly changes when I activate my lips and worship God. It becomes a joyful act even throughout suffering and it really is like medicine to the body. With Mum's situation, I had learnt from experience that worship was like a weapon that would not only help me but offer some kind of healing in the position we were in.

In the next chapter, I look at the thorn in Paul's side; he experienced suffering on his faith journey. He writes in 1 Thessalonians 5:16-18, "Rejoice always, pray continually, give thanks in all circumstances; for this is God's will for you in Christ Jesus."

These are crucial verses if you are to have a greater understanding of the life of faith. Keep your eyes on Jesus. Whatever life throws at you, always rejoice, give thanks and keep talking to God—this is God's will for your life. When we focus on Jesus, we are elevating Him in our lives and He is bigger than any problem, issue, trial, or cancer that we may come across in our lives.

There is a fourth and more striking similarity in these stories. Joshua and Jesus (in the second passage) had to see and give thanks for the supernatural outcome before it was a reality.

Chapter Four

Looking Into the Bible

I quote the Bible throughout this book. The reason for this is that the Bible has great significance in my journey. 2 Timothy 3:16-17 reads: "All Scripture is God-breathed and is useful for teaching, rebuking, correcting and training in righteousness, so that the servant of God may be thoroughly equipped for every good work."

This expresses the true value of the words written in this book. I believe that the Bible is God's Word to His people. It speaks into situations today. My experience is that if you are open to the Word of God and allow it, through the Spirit of God, it will breathe life into any situation or circumstance you face in your life today.

In Hebrews 4:12, we are told, "For the Word of God is alive and active. Sharper than any double-edged sword, it penetrates even to dividing soul and spirit, joints and marrow; it judges the thoughts and attitudes of the heart."

This is another huge claim which I believe. When we allow the Word of God to be activated in our lives as followers of Christ, we are allowing God to give us revelation instead of the confusion we may have from our own thoughts, feelings and understanding. We are able to distinguish God's purposes for our lives when we read and act upon the Living Word of God—the Bible.

In this chapter, I look at different examples from the Bible where it has helped direct my life, faith and understanding. The Bible has been fundamental to my journey of living with cancer and believing in and having understanding of God the Healer.

Prayer

I want to start by looking at how Jesus taught His followers to pray. Jesus tells us in Matthew 6:9-13:

"This, then, is how you should pray: 'Our Father in heaven, hallowed be your name, your kingdom come, your will be done, on earth as it is in heaven. Give us today our daily bread. And forgive us our debts, as we also have forgiven our debtors. And lead us not into temptation but deliver us from the evil one.'"

Prayer is conversation with God; conversation is a two-way process of both speaking and listening. God not only wants His followers to talk to Him but also to listen to Him. I believe that it is unlikely that Jesus wanted this to be only used as a word-for-word repetition prayer. Please notice the word "only" here. I am by no means saying that this shouldn't be prayed as it is; I often pray this prayer. But I believe Jesus was showing His followers, which includes those who follow Him today, areas that they need to cover in prayer. These areas include praise, a focus on God's kingdom purposes, obedience to God's will, provision for our needs, forgiveness and the need to avoid temptation in our lives. I am not going to cover all these areas in this book, but I want to look at two of the main points that Jesus is telling us to focus on when we pray and communicate with God.

The first one is praise, which to me speaks of devotion and worship. Jesus begins by telling us, "This, then, is how you should pray: 'Our Father in heaven, hallowed be your name.'" Jesus is telling us that the very first thing we should do in prayer is to give God praise. Sometimes we come to God in a desperate state and that's OK. But prayer and praise go together.

At our church, we have a service called 'Prayer and Praise'. We come together to praise God in worship through singing and we pray. Often, the things we pray for will come out of the time of worship, so we don't always have an agenda or a list of things we want to talk to God about. Something happens when our prayer times are focused on God and not on ourselves. This is why Jesus tells us to start our prayer times by giving God praise.

In anything we do, when we take the focus off Him, we miss the mark. We can do that in prayer—we can pray to God but make it about us, not Him. This is why Jesus taught us to keep the focus on God; He continues: "Our Father in heaven, hallowed be your name, your kingdom come, your will be done..."

It's all about Him. In the Old Testament part of the bible, in the first six verses of Psalm 95 it says:

> [1] Come, let us sing for joy to the LORD; let us shout aloud to the Rock of our salvation. [2] Let us come before Him with thanksgiving and extol Him with music and song.
>
> [3] For the LORD is the great God, the great King above all gods. [4] In His hand are the depths of the earth and the mountain peaks belong to Him. [5] The sea is His, for He made it and His hands formed the dry land.
>
> [6] Come, let us bow down in worship, let us kneel before the LORD our Maker.

I believe it is an example of how Jesus wants us to start our prayer times, by giving God some praise, giving Him the glory, giving Him what He deserves. When we do this, we are getting our priorities in place before we get into the details of our prayers. Jesus says later in Matthew 6:33, "But seek first His kingdom and His righteousness and all these things will be given to you as well." You see, when we put our focus on God and give Him what He deserves, other things often fall into place. To me, it is very clear that Jesus is guiding us to make sure that when we pray our focus is not on our circumstances or feelings but on God.

There is another point I want to look at in Jesus's teachings on how we should pray. This is something that I have missed for many years on my faith journey, but I think it is clearly referenced by Jesus here as a significant part of how we should pray: it is both OK and important to pray for ourselves.

After giving God the praise that He deserves, we are to pray: "Give us today our daily bread. And forgive us our debts, as we also have forgiven our debtors. And lead us not into temptation but deliver us from the evil one." Traditionally we have added, "For Thine is the kingdom, the power and the glory, for ever and ever. Amen"

If I look back on my prayer life, which has been very active for nearly forty years, I can be honest and say that the majority of my praying has been focused on praying for others. Again, being honest, I think that a large percentage of those prayers have been directly for my family: my parents, my wife, my children and my wider family. Additionally, I try to commit to pray for those who ask for prayer and those who I am aware that need prayer. This is all good and certainly not something I would discourage in anyone's prayer life. However, I am challenged by the recent revelation I have had from Jesus's direct instructions on how we should pray.

We have looked at the first section of the prayer that is focused on giving God praise when we pray, but the second half is centred around prayer for ourselves. This has struck a chord with me and has made me make recent adjustments to how I pray. I have a prayer wall in my study—I will be sharing more about what my prayer wall is later in this book. Basically, my prayer wall has lists of people and situations I am praying for. There are verses that I speak over my life which I referred to in chapter two. But I have recently added a section to my prayer wall that is very much focused on praying for me, which has been a direct response to what I believe Jesus is teaching His followers through The Lord's Prayer. Over the years I have had the misconception that it is selfish to pray for my own personal needs and is far more "spiritual" to pray for others.

Jesus's teaching in Matthew six is quite direct and seems to be equally split between focus on God and on our personal needs. These are very personal to the individual that is praying. Jesus instructs us to pray for daily needs like food, forgiveness (in different forms) and for strength to overcome life's temptations. I am also struck that there is no direct reference to praying for others in what we know as 'The Lord's Prayer'. Don't get me wrong, I have a long list of people and situations I pray for. That is right and there are plenty of biblical instructions for us to pray in this way, too. But the challenge for my own prayers, based on the Lord's Prayer, is firstly to honour God, give

Him praise and ultimately make my prayers more about Him than me.

Secondly, I must pray for myself. After all, I believe that in order for me to be as effective as I can as a follower of Jesus, I need to be in the best possible condition. Maybe, that is why Jesus teaches us to pray in this way. For example, if I am walking in obedience to God's purposes for my life. If I have my daily needs met, I am both forgiven and forgiving, able to resist temptations and evil influences over my life. Consequently, I am surely in the best place to be effective and have a positive influence in my life. There are other examples in the Bible where Jesus instructs His disciples to pray for themselves. If we are people of prayer this is a healthy discipline to have in our lives.

Faith

I want to look at two other passages from the Bible through the lens of faith: one from the Old Testament and one from the New Testament. Firstly, I want to look at one of my favourite passages in the Bible (Joshua 6:1-17a & 20):

> [1] Now the gates of Jericho were securely barred because of the Israelites. No one went out and no one came in.
>
> [2] Then the LORD said to Joshua, "See, I have delivered Jericho into your hands, along with its king and its fighting men. [3] March around the city once with all the armed men. Do this for six days. [4] Have seven

priests carry trumpets of rams' horns in front of the ark. On the seventh day, march around the city seven times, with the priests blowing the trumpets. **5** When you hear them sound a long blast on the trumpets, have the whole army give a loud shout; then the wall of the city will collapse and the army will go up, everyone straight in."

6 So Joshua, son of Nun, called the priests and said to them, "Take up the ark of the covenant of the LORD and have seven priests carry trumpets in front of it." **7** And he ordered the army, "Advance! March around the city, with an armed guard going ahead of the ark of the LORD."

8 When Joshua had spoken to the people, the seven priests carrying the seven trumpets before the LORD went forward, blowing their trumpets and the ark of the LORD's covenant followed them. **9** The armed guard marched ahead of the priests who blew the trumpets and the rear guard followed the ark. All this time the trumpets were sounding. **10** But Joshua had commanded the army, "Do not give a war cry, do not raise your voices, do not say a word until the day I tell you to shout. Then shout!" **11** So he had the ark of the LORD carried around the city, circling it once. Then the army returned to camp and spent the night there.

12 Joshua got up early the next morning and the priests took up the ark of the LORD. **13** The seven priests carrying the seven trumpets went forward, marching before the ark of the LORD and blowing the trumpets. The armed men went ahead of them and the rear guard followed the ark of the LORD, while the trumpets kept sounding. **14** So on the second day they marched around the city once and returned to the camp. They did this for six days.

15 On the seventh day, they got up at daybreak and marched around the city seven times in the same manner, except that on that day they circled the city seven times. **16** The seventh time around, when the priests sounded the trumpet blast, Joshua commanded the army, "Shout! For the LORD has given you the city! **17a** The city and all that is in it are to be devoted to the LORD...

20 When the trumpets sounded, the army shouted and at the sound of the trumpet, when the men gave a loud shout, the wall collapsed; so everyone charged straight in and they took the city.

The second passage is when Jesus feeds five thousand men, plus women and children. Matthew 14:13-21, reads:

13 When Jesus heard what had happened, He withdrew by boat privately to a solitary place. Hearing of this, the crowds followed Him on foot from the towns. **14** When Jesus landed and saw a large crowd, He had compassion on them and healed their sick.

15 As evening approached, the disciples came to Him and said, "This is a remote place and it's already getting late. Send the crowds away, so they can go to the villages and buy themselves some food."

16 Jesus replied, "They do not need to go away. You give them something to eat."

17 "We have here only five loaves of bread and two fish," they answered.

18 "Bring them here to me," He said. **19** And He directed the people to sit down on the grass. Taking the five loaves and the two fish and looking up to heaven, He gave thanks and broke the loaves. Then He gave them to the disciples and the disciples gave them to the people. **20** They all ate and were satisfied and the disciples picked up twelve basketfuls of broken pieces that were left over. **21** The number of those who ate was about five thousand men, besides women and children.

There are several different Bible passages that I could use to give the illustration I want to give here on the topic of faith. However, these passages work well, firstly because they are from totally different time zones: one was 1400 BC and the other in the period of AD27-30. And, secondly, because they offer consistencies in terms of how God can and does work.

The first similarity I want to make from these texts is that both situations seem to be impossible situations. Joshua and his army are trying to conquer Jericho and there is no way in: "The gates of Jericho were securely barred because of the Israelites. No one went out and no one came in." They don't seem to have the weaponry for the task, just a bunch of instruments.

In the second passage, there are five thousand hungry men, plus women and children, that all need feeding. They have five loaves of bread and two fish to feed all the people! These are both seemingly impossible situations where there is no obvious answer or way forward. Maybe we have experiences in life where we can relate to these situations? The problem seems to be far bigger than the situation we face. I know for myself personally that I regularly feel like this in different situations I face in life.

The second similarity in these passages and we only know this from reading the full accounts, is that they already had all they needed for the positive outcome. In Joshua's case, the army was big enough; they had all the musical instruments that were required; they had the ark; and they had their voices. In the second passage, they had the five loaves, two fish and the baskets that the food would be served in. In both situations, even though it didn't seem like it at the time, they already had all they needed for the positive outcome.

The third similarity is that they needed to act on what God was saying. Faith wasn't something that was limited to a feeling or a thought. It was an action, a doing, a march, a shout, a handing over, etc. Joshua had very specific instructions that involved marching for seven days, including a busy seventh day, playing their instruments and doing some shouting. In my opinion, Joshua had to demonstrate more faith and had it much tougher than the disciples because their act of obedience was to simply hand over the five loaves of bread and two fishes to Jesus.

There is a fourth and more striking similarity in these stories. Joshua and Jesus (in the second passage) had to see and give thanks for the supernatural outcome before it was a reality. Joshua was told by God (v2) before the walls came down and they could take Jericho: "See, I have delivered Jericho into your hands, along with its king and its fighting men." God then goes on to give Joshua the specific and somewhat strange, instructions that will make His promise become a reality for Joshua and his people. Joshua and his men had to act in the form of praise before the actual walls came down. This was an incredible act of obedience from Joshua. In the second passage, Jesus was now taking full responsibility: taking the five loaves and two fish and looking up to heaven, He gave thanks and broke the loaves. Then He gave them to the disciples and they gave them to the people. I suppose the challenge for the disciples was to start handing out what Jesus had given thanks for. I can't imagine this was like some kind of magic trick where suddenly hundreds of loaves and fish suddenly appeared. I imagine that, like the Joshua story, as the disciples began to hand out the food, it was amazing how it was distributed amongst thousands of people.

The Bible tells us in Hebrews 13:8 that Jesus Christ is the same yesterday and today and forever. I believe that through His followers, Jesus wants to demonstrate His power today, just as He did when He was on the earth. This is a staggering thought, one that is not easy for us to fully comprehend. But it is a consistent teaching throughout the Bible.

Jesus told us in John 14:12, "Very truly I tell you, whoever believes in me will do the works I have been doing and they will do even greater things than these, because I am going to the Father." We are also told in the first two verses of the book of John that Jesus is the Word and "in the beginning was the Word and the Word was with God and the Word was God". He was with God in the beginning. Therefore, we can assume that the supernatural expressions of God in the Old Testament are available to be expressed in and through Christ's followers today.

These first examples through Jesus's teaching us how to pray and how God can be used miraculously through His people are great and encouraging as we face different trials in our lives today. They offer us hope and reassurance in difficult circumstances. There is, however, a different perspective that I don't want to overlook in this book. This is the subject of suffering.

The reality of suffering

We have all experienced some kind of suffering; everyone suffers, everyone experiences some kind of physical or emotional pain, everyone experiences heartache, everyone gets ill and ultimately, everyone experiences death at some point. This is true throughout the teachings in the Bible. The Bible and the Christian journey is not some kind of life fix that leads to a bed of roses, or a life of freedom from all kinds of suffering or pain. If anyone says different, it's a false message. It would be unbalanced if I didn't look at the reality of suffering from a biblical perspective. So, in this section, I am going to look at some of what the Bible speaks of in terms of suffering.

The goal for a follower of Jesus is to live like Him. He is our ultimate example of how to live a godly life. So, there is no better way to start this by looking at Jesus. The prophet Isaiah speaks of the Jesus as the Suffering Servant in Isaiah 53:3-12:

³ He was despised and rejected by mankind, a man of suffering and familiar with pain. Like one from whom people hide their faces He was despised and we held Him in low esteem.

⁴ Surely, He took up our pain and bore our suffering, yet we considered Him punished by God, stricken by Him and afflicted.⁵   But He was pierced for our transgressions, He was crushed for our iniquities; the punishment that brought us peace was on Him and by His wounds we are healed.⁶ We all, like sheep, have gone astray, each of us has turned to our own way; and the LORD has laid on Him   the iniquity of us all.

⁷ He was oppressed and afflicted, yet He did not open His mouth; He was led like a lamb to the slaughter and as a sheep before its shearers is silent, so He did not open His mouth.⁸   By oppression and judgment He was taken away. Yet who of His generation protested? For He was cut off from the land of the living; for the transgression of my people, He was punished.⁹ He was assigned a grave with the wicked   and with the rich in His death, though He had done no violence, nor was any deceit in His mouth.

¹⁰ Yet it was the LORD's will to crush Him and cause Him to suffer and though the LORD makes His life an offering for sin, He will see His offspring and prolong His days and the will of the LORD will prosper in His hand.¹¹ After He has suffered,   He will see the light of life and be satisfied; by His knowledge my righteous servant will justify many and He will bear their iniquities.¹² Therefore I will give Him a portion among the great   and He will divide the spoils with the strong, because He poured out His life unto death   and was

numbered with the transgressors. For He bore the sin of many and made intercession for the transgressors.

In this passage, the prophet Isaiah gives us a detailed prophesy about the servant who was to experience intense suffering and die. The purpose of this was to take away the sin of the world. It is rather mind-blowing that this section of the Bible was found among the Dead Sea Scrolls and therefore written over seven hundred years prior to Jesus's crucifixion. I am happy to claim that the "servant" described is unquestionably Jesus Christ. This chapter in Isaiah is also related to Jesus on many occasions in the New Testament. There is no doubt that Jesus suffered; the challenge for us can be found in 1 Peter 2:21 where we are told this: "To this you were called because Christ suffered for you, leaving you an example, that you should follow in His steps." The injustice Jesus suffered on our behalf will never be matched with what injustices we will suffer. But we should not be surprised if we suffer and are treated in an unjust manner, as we live in a fallen and unjust world! In fact, Jesus tells us in Matthew 16:24: "Whoever wants to be my disciple must deny themselves and take up their cross and follow me." This is the cost for every follower of Jesus; in most of our lives we won't have to suffer remotely what Jesus did but there is a cost, there is an element of suffering. To ignore this would be like having an unbalanced diet that leads to an unhealthy lifestyle. If I am to pick up my cross and follow Jesus, there is no doubt that the journey will not always be smooth. Actually, it will be quite a challenging journey; lots of sweat, discomfort, struggle and pain.

Another passage I want to look at in terms of the subject of suffering is the very well-known Psalm of David, Psalm 23:

> [1] The LORD is my shepherd, I lack nothing. [2] He makes me lie down in green pastures, He leads me beside quiet waters, [3] He refreshes my soul. He guides me along the right paths for His name's sake. [4] Even though I walk through the darkest valley, I will fear no evil, for you are with me; your rod and your staff, they comfort me.
>
> [5] You prepare a table before me   in the presence of my enemies. You anoint my head with oil; my cup overflows. [6] Surely your goodness and love will follow me all the days of my life and I will dwell in the house of the LORD forever.

Sandwiched in the middle of this Psalm are the words "even though I walk through the darkest valley..." These words are sandwiched between great promises of God providing our needs, guiding us on the right paths and God anointing us to overflowing and eternal promises. It cannot be ignored that some sort of pain and suffering are to be expected for us in this life. This is not so much a possibility, rather an inevitability. But the great news is that in those certain times of suffering, we do not need to fear because God is with us during those seasons in our lives. Not only is God with us, but He promises to comfort us and bless us in those seasons of our lives. Again, this is a reality that we cannot hide from: that there will be some sort of suffering at times in our lives. When I look back at times of suffering in my life God has used them for personal growth. Maybe that is why in James 1:2-4 we are told to "Consider it pure joy, my brothers and sisters, whenever you face trials of many kinds, because you know that the testing of your faith produces perseverance. Let perseverance finish its work so that you may be mature and complete, not lacking anything". Notice that here we are told "whenever" we face trials "of many kinds". This is not something we can avoid in this life.

The final passage I want to look at is 2 Corinthians 12:1-10. St Paul, the writer, shares a vision about a thorn in his side. This is ultimately about Paul's dependence on God's strength in suffering:

> "I must go on boasting. Although there is nothing to be gained, I will go on to visions and revelations from the Lord. I know a man in Christ who fourteen years ago was caught up to the third heaven. Whether it was in the body or out of the body I do not know—God knows. And I know that this man—whether in the body or apart from the body I do not know, but God knows — was caught up to paradise and heard inexpressible things, things that no one is permitted to tell. I will boast about a man like that, but I will not boast about myself, except about my weaknesses. Even if I should choose to boast, I would not be a fool, because I would be speaking the truth. But I refrain, so no one will think more of me than is warranted by what I do or say, or because of these surpassingly great revelations. Therefore, in order to keep me from becoming conceited, I was given a thorn in my flesh, a messenger of Satan, to torment me. Three times I pleaded with the Lord to take it away from me. But He said to me, 'My grace is sufficient for you,

for my power is made perfect in weakness.' Therefore, I will boast all the more gladly about my weaknesses, so that Christ's power may rest on me. That is why, for Christ's sake, I delight in weaknesses, in insults, in hardships, in persecutions, in difficulties. For when I am weak, then I am strong."

For the purpose of this book, there is no point speculating what the thorn is in Paul's side; he doesn't state the identity of it and different theologians have made cases for the thorn representing different things. The point is that this was a thorn in his side. It was uncomfortable, it caused Paul pain and was something that he pleaded with God to remove. I think it is fair to say that you wouldn't plead with God over something that was a mild hindrance; this would have caused Paul great suffering.

Paul was a hugely significant figure in the days of the early church; he was radically transformed from murdering followers of Christ to making them followers. He was responsible for opening the door of the Christian faith to the Gentiles and for being inspired to write most of the New Testament. We cannot underestimate the significance of Paul's influence. Yet, incredibly, he had this constant battle with a certain suffering. Jesus told Paul "His grace was sufficient for him, for my power is made perfect in weakness". Paul's response to this revelation was amazing; and something we can learn from in our times of suffering. What an incredible heart Paul had for God that he should rejoice in suffering and rejection, lack, oppression and other difficulties. What a difference with those that whinge and whine when exposed to hardship!

Paul faces his negative situation and transforms it into a positive one. What a great example for us when we face trials.

Jesus trained His disciples to think supernaturally and not limit God by rational thinking. We saw an example of that in the previous chapter, when we looked at the feeding of the five thousand. Faith enlarges our minds to think past the limits of natural thinking.

Chapter Five

But It's Not Easy

If you are still with me, you will know that I am a Christian who believes that healing, even from terminal illnesses, is possible today. That is clear from the back cover. I do believe this and have already explained that I have had personal experience of this. But the truth is believing this can also be a struggle—it's not easy!

Six years ago, it was very rare for me to take any medication. As I write this, I have a thirty-six litre plastic box that is full of some of my daily medication. I go into hospital every three weeks for an injection that helps stabilise the tumours that are in my body. If you are squeamish about injections, then this one is not for you: it's a significant size of needle and can be quite painful. The injection and the endless number of tablets (over forty a day) are a constant reminder that there is something wrong.

There is a certain tablet that I must take with anything that I eat; so I can't go anywhere without making sure I have my tablets. I am not entirely sure if these tablets are directly related to the cancer, but in my head they are as I never took medication before I was diagnosed and had surgery. The point is that numerous times a day, I am reminded of the medical condition due to the ongoing medication. This is, of course, true for anyone who takes medication for any kind of situation. My experience of this is two-fold in that I am truly thankful for the medication that I can take to help with a variety of things. But I have often struggled with the amount of medication that I must take. Since my original diagnosis the amount of medication I take has consistently increased due to the catalogue of diagnoses that have followed.

There was a time when I had a stint in hospital for a recurring bout of chronic pancreatitis and they found a clot. This resulted in an additional two tablets per day for the rest of my life. It was expressed to me how important it was to take the tablets and that they were potentially life-saving due to my situation. Even in writing this, I am thinking I would have been filled with gratitude that not only was this identified, but that this medication was also available to me. Nor to mention that because I was a cancer patient, I don't pay for my prescriptions, for which I am truly thankful. At the time, my feeling was not of gratitude, it was quite the opposite. I felt depressed at the thought of more medication; I felt vulnerable at the thought of having to rely on tablets in order to thin my blood; I felt sorry for myself and incredibly frustrated by the situation I was in. In many ways, this makes me feel uncomfortable writing this. I feel I should have been thankful that I was in the privileged situation to get this information about what was going on in my body, that medication was identified that would help me long term and that this medication was so easily accessible for me. Wow! What a privileged situation to be in. Yet I was incredibly low by the reminder of my cancerous condition.

The truth is that I hate the amount of medication I have to take. It drives me crazy and is a constant reminder of the negative circumstance in my life. I appreciate that some people will understand this while some will think that I am fortunate to be in this position. There isn't a right or wrong response to this. My point, however, is that (as I shared in chapter two) I believe my response to the situation I am in is ultimately down to choice. I can look at my medication situation and feel sorry for myself. I can be troubled by the reminder of my diagnosis or diagnoses. I can wonder why there isn't a medication that attacks the type of cancer I have. Alternatively, I could be incredibly thankful that we have a system in the country I was fortunate to live in that has identified my condition. I can be thankful that I have expert doctors to support me and provide medication to slow down the growth of my tumours. When I look back over the time of my diagnosis, I have been in both of these camps. Some days it is very difficult, but it is always to my mental advantage when I take my medication; I try to do this with a positive outlook, being thankful.

The medication is only one aspect of the challenge. It is the same with every trip to the hospital, regular scans, appointments and very regular trips to the pharmacy to collect prescriptions. Looking at my diary today, I have three hospital appointments next week and, I have to say, this doesn't fill me with excitement. Once you get into the regular routine of these things it just becomes part of life. But just like taking medication, they are a gentle reminder of the cancer.

Sometimes the scans are quite difficult. Waiting for the cannulas to be inserted has become quite an ordeal as it regularly takes four or five attempts because my veins have weakened over time. But the waiting and process of the scan going through the machine is an obvious reminder that is slapping you full on in the face. This really can be a battle of the mind; and I am fully aware that I have it very easy compared to some that I have met in hospital.

I had no idea when I set out to write this book that I would be writing this for my benefit as well as others; but the reality is that I am finding it very helpful to write this down as a reminder of the blessings I have and the things I should be thankful for. It is true that in any trial of life, it takes a disciplined mind to focus on the positives rather than the pain of the trial. It's not easy.

One thing I was told when I was first diagnosed is the type of cancer I have is very rare and not many people (including doctors) knew a great deal about it. So, I was encouraged to make sure I checked everything I was told through my specialist as other professional doctors could tell me things in error. Over the last six years, I have found this to be incredibly useful information.

An example of this was during the first pandemic in 2020. I had to have my injections delivered to my home for me to self-inject. This wasn't too much of a problem for me and I soon got used to doing them. That Christmas, I had given myself the injection and a few days later I had a considerable growth on the area I injected. This was alarming and painful. I went to the hospital and they were very concerned. My specialist team were not in the hospital and were not going to be in for a few days. I can remember it like it was yesterday: a consultant came into my hospital room to see me. His manner, tone and everything about him was incredibly sympathetic towards my situation.

At this point, I was reasonably confident that the swelling had been caused by the injection that I had administered to myself only a few days earlier. And I was also aware that the consultant was not in the department of expertise for my type of cancer. He looked at me and began to talk to me about my three children at home. He told me that I needed to go home and spend twenty-four hours with my children before coming back into hospital when they would know more about what to do. He was, without spelling it out, telling me that I needed to go home and spend some final hours with my family as it was likely that the cause of the lump was the cancer spreading. That feeling, that moment was chilling and it will stay with me forever. In one sense I was conscious that I really needed to speak to one of my specialists, but I was also conscious that when my type of cancer begins to flare up, it does so aggressively. Thankfully, when I got home one of my specialists had heard about the situation and contacted me to reassure me that they were very sure that the growth was unrelated to the cancer.

On another occasion, I was in hospital having an ultrasound. The person doing the procedure was looking at the screen and looked horrified at what they saw. Again, I can remember this clearly as I write. In a strange sense, the expression of horror was quite comical, due to the obviousness of it. However, the reality for my heart was that it was alarming. Of course, it resulted in me being very nervous. I can remember saying, "It is clear something is wrong, what was it?" My anxiety increased dramatically when I didn't get an immediate response. After this delay, that probably felt longer than it was, I exclaimed, "Please, tell me what's wrong!" The response was, "I am sorry I need to go get someone else, I will be back soon." Then the person left the room.

The following few minutes felt like an hour. I was frightened, confused, thinking about Lucy and the children. The mind goes crazy in these kinds of circumstances. The bizarre thing about this was that when the more senior member of staff came back with the original person, they both looked at the screen and looked horrified. The senior person turned to me and said: "Do you know what you have"? So, I began to explain about my diagnosis of carcinoid syndrome (the cancer). Surprisingly, as I explained, there was a sense of relief on their faces. It turned out that they had not seen my notes before I went in for the ultrasound. I can only presume that they thought they were about to inform me that I had a rare type of cancer that I didn't already know about. I am not sure who was more relieved in that room once we all knew what was going on.

The truth is that after incidences like this (I could share more) you must quickly pick yourself up and be positive, otherwise you can feel down very quickly. Apart from my faith, my children—Jessica, Luke and Sophie—are incredibly influential on me, helping me dig deep and be positive during my trials. In this situation with the ultrasound, I didn't have time to feel sorry for myself or get dragged down by the sudden anxiety that I experienced in that room. This was because I was late for a planned Face Time with my children, so as soon as I got back to the ward, I Face Timed them. This was not a time for me to offload that anxiety onto my children, I had to be strong and positive.

It is not just the medication and the hospital experiences that are not easy. I have found that the most difficult thing is controlling my mind. In chapter two, when I talked about choosing your identity, I shared the following Bible verse: "Take captive every thought to make it obedient to Christ" (2 Corinthians 10:5). This verse has become part of my daily life since my diagnosis. In some ways, it is an error on my part because the verse is not limited to those with terminal illnesses; it's a verse that is essential for all of us that are followers of Jesus.

If we don't have relationship with Jesus and keep looking to Him through the Word of God and through His Spirit, then we are limited to natural thinking. Examples of these thoughts could be: "I am not good enough"; "They won't listen to me"; "I can't write a book"; "I won't live long enough to see my daughter get married"; or "I won't see my grandchildren." As you can imagine, some of these are regular thoughts of mine. Not all our thoughts are bad or negative, but many are. The point of this verse about taking our thoughts captive and making them obedient to Christ it is to align our thinking with what Christ says and thinks about us. Jesus trained His disciples to think supernaturally and not limit God by rational thinking. We saw an example of that in the previous chapter, when we looked at the feeding of the five thousand. Faith enlarges our minds to think past the limits of natural thinking.

In concluding this chapter, I am reminded of the old BT commercials where we were told, "It's Good to Talk." It is good for us to have people we can speak to about our fears, struggles, doubts and temptations. The advantage of having a relationship with God is that we have the ultimate Counsellor already in place. Jesus told us in John

14:16-17, "And I will ask the Father and He will give you another Advocate to help you and be with you forever—the Spirit of Truth. The world cannot accept Him, because it neither sees Him nor knows Him. But you know Him, for He lives with you and will be in you." This is such a wonderful promise for followers of Jesus, of all generations.

The Advocate is the Counsellor, the Spirit of Truth. As believers in Jesus, when we communicate with Him, we are communicating with the Great Counsellor who can give us revelation through His Word. This is wonderful and is a reality for all those in relationship with God; but it is also essential for us to be able to talk with trusted people about our trials. I mentioned a moment ago about how I couldn't remain in the state of anxiousness I was in while having the ultrasound. This was because I was having a Face Time conversation with my children. This was good for me in the sense that I had purpose and a desire not to stay in that place of anxiety. So, picking myself up and being positive helped me. But this didn't stop me expressing my anxiety about that situation to Lucy later. It was important for me to do that.

Sometimes, life can be horribly tough; to say that sometimes "it is not easy" can be an understatement. But it is "good to talk" and share our weaknesses. In Ephesians 3:12, we are told, "In Him and through faith in Him we may approach God with freedom and confidence." The advantage of talking to God is that we can speak about anything, there is nothing He can't handle. It is totally right that we share and seek out people who we can confide in—that is not in question at all. But it is important that we don't get into a pattern of drifting from speaking to the One who is available at all times.

CANCER AND THE CROSS

People are very open to people who hold onto their faith from a place of suffering.

Chapter Six

Can Good Come from Cancer?

It feels quite a strange thing to say, but in many ways, especially for my walk of faith, my diagnosis has been the "kick up the backside" that I needed. It wasn't an immediate thought. In fact, my immediate thought was more like "this is the kick in the teeth that I didn't need". I am in no way whatsoever thankful for the cancer. But as I look back, I can say that as well as it causing great physical and mental pain, there are aspects of the diagnosis that have had a positive influence over my life. I don't see the cancer as positive at all; but I am aware that as a result of the cancer, it has led to positive things. Of course, one of those things will hopefully be this book! This chapter explores answers to the question: can good come from cancer? My life experiences suggest that it can.

The first example of this is that I don't want to hold grudges and want to be right with people, because you simply don't know how long you have. This is not to say that prior to my diagnosis I had many grudges and didn't get on with people—far from it. But I am now more conscious of being in good relationships with people and feel the need to resolve any differences. It is not always easy but, according to Jesus, it is paramount for followers of Him: "For if you forgive other people when they sin against you, your heavenly Father will also forgive you. But if you do not forgive others their sins, your Father will not forgive your sins" (Matthew 6:14-15 NIV).

This teaching from Jesus is not up for debate amongst His followers; it is not a "grey" area, it is strong and clear. Because He is so forgiving to us, we are to be forgiving to others. The consequences of failing to forgive are catastrophic. The strength of Jesus's teaching on this subject is so strong that I feel somewhat embarrassed that it took a terminal diagnosis to consider it in depth. The truth is that forgiveness is a fundamental aspect of our lives. Forgiveness and being right with people can sometimes be a process and at times is even out of our control; however, the desire to be right with people is something that has increased since my diagnosis.

It is not only my desire to be in right relationship with people that has progressed; it is also my desire to be right with God. It wasn't that I was in a bad place from a relationship with God prior to my diagnosis, I don't believe I was. I suppose what has happened is that I am increasingly aware of my own weaknesses—and more aware of the need of God's power in my life. In a strange sense, I have found that when you experience frailties of your body, it has made certain biblical truths easier to grasp.

For example, 2 Corinthians 12:10 says, "That is why, for Christ's sake, I delight in weaknesses, in insults, in hardships, in persecutions, in difficulties. For when I am weak, then I am strong." What I have found is that my personal weaknesses have elevated my dependence on God's strength in my life.

In Colossians 1:26-27, we are told of a wonderful promise to followers of Jesus: "The mystery that has been kept hidden for ages and generations but is now disclosed to the Lord's people. To them, God has chosen to make known among the Gentiles the glorious riches of this mystery, which is Christ in you, the hope of glory."

This is one of the greatest and most staggering promises in the Bible. It's a revelation that is for every believer: that Jesus Christ lives in them, through His Spirit and that He is the hope of glory for all eternity. Wow, what an incredible promise! I believed this well before I was diagnosed but the advantage of having an affliction, I have found, is that it has caused me to rely on God's strength within me more regularly. Basically, the disease has intensified my personal battle which has driven me to look to God more regularly for empowerment.

Another example is that Philippians 4:13 tells me "I can do all this through Him who gives me strength". Again, my weakness highlights the need for strength from elsewhere. A danger for us, when we don't have obvious frailties, is that we can become reliant on our own strengths and abilities. In effect, my diagnosis has opened the door for me to ask for and seek, more of God's presence, power and strength in my life. My weakness is almost becoming my strength in that I am becoming increasingly dependent on God due to my diagnosis. In a bizarre way, I am thankful for my situation and can relate completely to Paul's claim in 2 Corinthians 12:10: "That is why, for Christ's sake, I delight in weaknesses, in insults, in hardships, in persecutions, in difficulties. For when I am weak, then I am strong."

Another example of a positive outcome from my diagnosis is that I now have a far greater desire to make the most of every opportunity. That includes events that we may see as small, simple things: being extra friendly to people, letting people in and out while driving, opening doors for others, being polite, picking up litter when walking... Don't get me wrong, I am not out every day clearing up the community, but I have a greater sense of taking up the opportunity to do the right thing.

To be fair, I think many smaller acts are something I would do prior to my diagnosis; however, the urgency to be kind and do the right thing has intensified in my life. It really is true that we don't know what is going on in people's lives. I have become increasingly aware that when you suffer, it is inevitable that you go through times of feeling very low. In those times, I have experienced the kindness of others pulling me up and offering me encouragement. It is often through random acts of kindness from people who don't know my situation. I don't think we realise how powerful this can be. It can transform someone's day, bring them out of depression and even draw them to God. If there is any way I can do this by showing simple acts of kindness, I want to do that.

One thing that has undoubtedly developed in my life since my diagnosis is that I have a greater urge to share my faith. Again, I have always been a bit of an evangelist. Sharing my faith has always been a part of my life but there was an instant injection of necessity within me once cancer became a reality. The truth is that I really believe what Jesus said in John 14:6: "I am the way and the truth and the life. No one comes to the Father except through me". You see, if you believe those words and you can't access God without going through Jesus, then knowing and hearing about Jesus is paramount for everyone. There are eternal consequences that, if I am honest, I was far too comfortable about prior to my diagnosis. I am not saying we all need some kind of diagnosis or disaster to take place in our lives to wake us up, but it does feel a little like that for me as I look back. I am now always looking out for opportunities to share what I believe is the greatest gift you can give anyone: introducing them to Jesus.

Not only has my diagnosis given me a deeper desire to share my faith, but I am also far more confident in doing so. This is because I am coming from it in a place of pain, a place where everything isn't "hunky-dory" for me—life is tough. I have found that sharing faith from that place is very effective. People are very open to people who hold onto their faith from a place of suffering.

I am currently on the longest run of avoiding a prolonged stay in hospital, which I am thankful for. The last four years have been incredibly challenging, with many trips in and out of hospital. I have found myself depressed by the thought of going back into hospital while also having a genuine sense of excitement because I know that when I go into hospital, I will get the opportunity to share my faith. I want to share some of my experiences while being in hospital.

Two hospital encounters

It was nearing midnight and most people on my side of the ward were settling down to sleep. Due to the pandemic, the beds were about three metres apart and when nurses came to speak to you, they did it from a bit of a distance. It meant it was quite loud on the ward as people spoke loudly to be heard. The man next to me had a serious foot infection and was rolling about in agony for some time. You could hear and sense others on the ward becoming agitated as they couldn't sleep due to the noise the man was making. I prayed for him in my bed and sensed that God was asking me the question, "Why don't you pray for him?" It seemed quite strange as I was praying for him and God knew it. But I knew straight away what God was getting at: it was clear that God wanted me to be a bit bolder and offer to pray with the man.

My problem was I knew this would disturb others and they would see what was going on. So, I reluctantly sat up and in a strong whisper—not wanting anyone else to hear —said something like, "Can I pray for you? I am a vicar." I don't normally identify myself as a vicar, I am a church minister or pastor, but I thought a vicar was more recognisable than my other options.

The man replied, in a much louder voice than mine, "What? I can't hear you!" Then I remembered that earlier this man had told me he was a retired professional speedway driver and it had significantly affected his hearing. I knew I was fully in now, there was no going back as the man repeated, "What? I can't hear you!"

I got a little bolder and repeated, "I can tell you are in pain; can I pray for you? I am a vicar." I could tell others on the ward heard but, again, my hospital friend replied, "I still can't hear you!" My attempts couldn't continue, so I made sure he would hear this time: "I CAN TELL YOU

ARE IN PAIN; CAN I PRAY FOR YOU? I AM A VICAR!" He
heard all right—as did all the other men on the ward.

The man responded very positively to me. Before I
prayed, I quickly scanned the room and saw three of the
men who were, a moment ago, trying to sleep. They
stared at me, waiting to see what I was going to do. I
watched another place his book down and look over
intently—whether I liked it or not, I had people's attention.
I had to pray quickly as I began to get nervous and my
intention was to pray privately. I knew I had to pray loudly
as I didn't want to go through what had just happened.
So, with the onlookers, I prayed a loud and simple prayer
asking God to heal the man and take the pain from him.
The man was thankful for the prayer and others began to
lay back down wondering what had just happened.

A few minutes passed and there was a noticeable
difference in the room. The noises of pain and discomfort
were no longer heard. So, I asked the man, "How's the
pain?" I had forgotten about his deafness! He replied,
"What? I can't hear you!" As the volume increased, others
began to listen again. The man announced: "I can't
believe it! I have no idea what you have done but the pain
has gone, thank you." Everyone heard.

At that moment a nurse walked into the ward and walked
over to the man I had just prayed for. "It's time for your
pain relief," she said. He replied, "I am not sure I need it,
that man has done a job on me and his words have taken
the pain away." He didn't get any more pain relief that
night and we all had a good sleep. The man went into
hospital to have his leg amputated but left with both legs
and an incredible experience of God's healing. To my
knowledge he still has both his legs. The amazing thing

was, that it wasn't just the man that experienced that, it was all the men on the ward and also the staff.

On another occasion, 5 February 2021, I had been in accident and emergency for nearly thirty hours. I was in considerable pain and the stress levels in the hospital were like I have never known. This was mainly down to the recent pandemic. I had never sensed an atmosphere like it on the numerous visits I have had to hospital. It was a strange combination of great love and commitment from staff, who all seemed to be carrying a great pressure from their workload and constant stress levels from both the staff and patients. It was a mixture of lots of love, frustration, understanding, some anger, tears of both stress and pain and fear from staff and patients.

Due to the lack of sleep, no food for days, being in considerable pain and worrying about what was wrong with me, I was desperate to get to my hospital bed, which had been on the cards for the last eighteen hours. I had already been made aware that my stay in hospital was going to be for several days. But such was the need for bed space throughout the hospital, one didn't come forward quickly. That was until 11:30am—the day after and twenty-eight hours since my admission. This bed was going to be made available by 1:15pm. I can remember starting to cry with relief as the physical pain and discomfort was so tangible.

The timings are key to this story, as people were placed in certain positions at just the right time, so that God could work. I didn't realise it at the time, however! At 12pm, I was wheeled right next to the exit of the treatment area of A&E. I was ready to go, had my bed overloaded with all my belongings, was desperate to leave the chaos of A&E and get some appropriate pain relief and treatment. I had only been there for thirty-seconds when a young man, who was clearly suffering, was wheeled into the bay opposite me. This area was cramped; nurses and doctors worked frantically in between each bed. Thankfully, a nurse went to see the young man and closed his curtains, I say thankfully because I simply didn't have the strength to communicate with him. I had already had several faith conversations and didn't think I could handle any more.

As the nurse began to speak to this young man, however, it was clear God was prompting me to talk to this young man about Jesus. The reason why it was so obvious was that there was lots of movement, busyness and conversations going on at the same time; yet, suddenly, I could only hear the conversation with the nurse and the young man. I really didn't want to hear what I was hearing and, at one point, I even tried to cover my ears. It didn't work and I just knew God was preparing an opportunity for a conversation. I can be honest and say I thought, "Not now God, give me a break."

I will not go into the details of the conversation between the nurse and the young man, but his life situation was incredibly messy and he needed some help. The issue was that he was reluctant to give any contact details to the nurse who was offering him help. I knew exactly what he needed and at that moment, I didn't want another missed opportunity on my list. I knew if I was going to make a move, I had to be quick, but time wasn't on my side. It had passed 1:15pm and I was due to be wheeled off any minute. Just then, the curtains opened and the nurse went off in one direction and the young man went for a shower. I sensed my opportunity had gone, but immediately a doctor came to me and said that my blood pressure had increased too much for me to leave and I couldn't go until it was reduced. This was the first moment I was OK about the delay. I had gone from having tears of joy that I was moving on from A&E to being thankful that my high blood pressure was keeping me in.

During the conversation between the nurse and the young man, I heard pretty much every word, despite it being a noisy area. Without thinking, I shouted for the nurse while the young man was showering. I didn't know what to say when she got to me, so blurted out, "Sorry, I couldn't help overhearing your conversation opposite. I can help him, but I am due to be wheeled off soon". Thankfully, she didn't dismiss me as a crazy man and, out of concern for him, wanted a better explanation from me. Having proved I was a church pastor and explained that I had experience of working with people in similar situations to this young man, she agreed that it would be helpful we spoke. But she basically said, "I appreciate you are clearly unwell yourself, but you need to find a way in to get him onside, he won't give me the information I need to help him". So, my prayer was simple: "God, give me a way in if you want me to help him."

The strangest thing happened. The vast majority of times, when God speaks it is like feelings or ideas that drop in my mind. I was certain it was God speaking when I immediately thought I should ask the young man if he knew two people I knew. This was a pretty specific word; I was about to ask someone I never met if he knew two people I knew. In fairness, there was a slim chance as they were similar ages and one had lived in the same town, which has a population of over twenty-two thousand people. It was certainly an outside chance and I didn't have a back-up plan if his answer was, "No."

Anyway, I was obedient and as he came out of the shower, although I felt uneasy, I was shocked by my confidence. I didn't ask him if he knew anyone, but simply put to him where did he know the two men from. Instantly, I had this young man's full attention; you could see in his face expression that God had given me my way in. He came over, sat on my bed and shook my hand. It was in the times we were supposed to keep a distance and certainly not touch each other. He wanted to know how I knew that he knew the two other men. Without hesitation, but maybe again feeling a little uneasy, I told him that God had told me because He wanted us to talk. I began to tell him that I was a local pastor and could help him. I wasn't speaking for long before I noticed his eyes well up. Suddenly, this tough man was crying on my bed and others noticed.

To my surprise, he began to explain how he gave his life to Jesus several years ago in prison but had turned his back on God when his dad died. His life was broken in many ways, but he was amazed how God had placed me in that situation to speak to him. He was as convinced, as was I, that he was in the middle of a move of God. He explained how the last week was one of the worst weeks of his life and at this point, he was really on the edge. Over the last, God had been on his mind a few times, but he felt it was too late for him and that there was no way back and God wouldn't take him back. On his way into hospital, he gave God an ultimatum: "Reveal Yourself to me and I will sort my life out!"

This really was an incredible moment. We were both crying. God was reaching out His hand to this broken, young man. I took a moment to pray for him in front of several staff, who stood still in acknowledgement and after refusing to give his number to others, we had each other's number and were connected. At that very moment, two porters came to wheel me away without taking my blood pressure. It is truly amazing how God finds a way to reach His children, what an expression of love from God to this young man! I was in a desperate state myself but also thankful I was able to be used like that to help this young man.

The cancer has had many negative influences on my life. The physical and emotional pain have been so tough at times. The impact on family life has not been easy. It has also had a negative impact on my work as a church pastor, especially in terms of time off and having times of low energy. But I also believe positives have emerged from this cancer in terms of my work. This is not only true for the examples I have given, especially the point of having increased influence ministering from a place of pain. But I believe and sometimes hear that my preaching has improved.

Preaching

In the Old Testament—Exodus 4:10-12—Moses is having an encounter with God through a burning bush. God asks Moses to speak to Pharaoh on behalf of God's people so that they can be freed from slavery; Moses has some reservations and he responds to God: "Pardon your servant, Lord. I have never been eloquent, neither in the past nor since you have spoken to your servant. I am slow of speech and tongue. The LORD said to him, 'Who gave human beings their mouths? Who makes them deaf or mute? Who gives them sight or makes them blind? Is it not I, the LORD? **12** Now go; I will help you speak and will teach you what to say.'"

I can understand Moses's reservations, even though my responsibilities are nothing like his in this instance. I recognise the pressures of speaking God's Word. It has always been something I take very seriously and sometimes feel out of my depth when having the responsibility of it. Why would God choose me? I am not a naturally gifted speaker but as someone that has chosen this path and feels called to it, I have a responsibility in it.

In my first five years of being a minister, I grew in confidence as a speaker as I spoke every week in a public setting. There were trials as I grew and had to deal with uncertain health and pain issues that were not identified by my doctor. But once I was officially diagnosed and that became increasingly public, it seemed to be different. As I said earlier, I wasn't preaching from a place of comfort. I was preaching from a place of suffering. This made my words increasingly more effective and spoke into the reality of the situations of those to whom I was speaking. The sense of "it's ok for you" or "yes, but the reality of life for us is pain" was departing. I was speaking as someone who knew the realities of life. My voice became increasingly effective.

Like Moses, I didn't feel that I wasn't an eloquent speaker or had good speech. If I am honest, I didn't feel as though my tongue was useful to God in terms of preaching. I knew many other people with a more eloquent and sufficient voice that could be used more powerfully than mine. But as God said to Moses, it wasn't about my abilities, it was more about my willingness. I was ready to be used by God in whatever ways He wanted to use me.

After responding to this call, I saw God use my voice, but I think my diagnosis dramatically improved it. I became far more confident in being direct instead of trying to persuade people with my voice. I did this while also having a greater sensitivity to those who may be listening while going through a challenging time. I also found that, or it certainly felt like, I could get people's attention. I think this was down to the fact that my life experiences were real and not from a place of theory. In a strange way, it felt like my diagnosis gave me the right to speak. One thing I can say with assurance, however, is that when I got diagnosed, I stopped spending time getting to the point I wanted to make. I started saying things as they were. In truth, I became less interested in pleasing people and far more conscious in pleasing God with my words. I believe the authority in my preaching stepped up to another level. Don't get me wrong here, I certainly don't see myself as a special speaker. I consider myself very average and know many people who are far more gifted in this area. I just believe that my diagnosis helped elevate my preaching to a higher level. My absolute priority is to get the message that God wants me to get across out there. I will certainly do that at the cost of embarrassing myself or putting myself in a situation where I must rely on God to use my voice.

In concluding this chapter, I want to look to the words of Timothy, in 2 Timothy 4:2. He tells us to "preach the word; be prepared in season and out of season; correct, rebuke and encourage—with great patience and careful instruction". I always considered myself as preaching with encouragement and patience. My diagnosis has helped me add the other aspects of this verse to develop my preaching.

I know that every time Liz left her house to go for a walk, she didn't necessarily feel like smiling.

But just like a hat or some shoes, Liz chose to put on joy and to put on a smile.

Chapter Seven
Faith Shines Through: Death is NOT Defeat!

In chapter two, I told you a story about how I was walking past a local pub and thought about who would take my son for his first pint. This hit me hard, even though I had never previously thought about taking my nine-year-old for a beer. Moments after this cutting thought, I got a text message from someone that transformed my mentality from a negative one to a positive one. I want to introduce you to Liz, who I have dedicated this book to and who sent me that text that transformed my mindset that morning.

Liz lost her battle with cancer in 2022 and I had the privilege of taking a service of thanksgiving for her life in November 2022. Liz was a remarkable woman who had a deep impact on my life. She was a dear friend and a member of my congregation. She was diagnosed with terminal cancer in February 2014 and the prognosis was not good. I remember the day clearly when her husband, Steve, called to give me the news. It was devastating. Remarkably, Liz's journey was a great example to many as she lived her life with her diagnosis while having a strong conviction that she would be healed. In many ways, Liz showed me how to live a life with a terminal diagnosis, while also having faith in her God. This chapter is dedicated to Liz and her family as I share how she inspired me in my journey.

There is little point ignoring the challenging questions straight away. One of the big questions that we face here is how this can be a positive example in the context of this book if Liz ultimately died from cancer. We will look at this at the conclusion of this chapter when we see that "death is not a defeat".

Firstly, I want to focus on the incredible example I took from how Liz lived her life. After about a year into her illness, Liz was installed as an elder (leader) within the church. This was quite an unusual situation as with ongoing health issues, it wasn't necessarily an obvious thing to do. However, the way Liz lived her life made this an obvious choice, simply because of the example she set: living her life the way she did made her very influential. There is a verse in the Bible that highlights this and I want this chapter to focus on the three main conditions from 1 Thessalonians 5:16-18: "Rejoice always, pray continually, give thanks in all circumstances; for this is God's will for you in Christ Jesus."

These verses are vitally important for keeping a life of faith. We have a church statement that declares "Love, Live and Share Jesus". The verses in 1 Thessalonians show us how to keep our focus on Jesus, no matter what the circumstances we face in life. Always rejoice, be thankful and continue to pray; this is what the Bible says is God's will for us. It is not that if you are a person of faith in Jesus you don't have problems, far from it. But faith in Jesus raises you above your problems, opposition and needs because, as Christians, we believe we already have every blessing in Christ (Ephesians 1:3).

Rejoice always

Despite her circumstances, Liz seemed to be full of joy. She was always rejoicing, always had a smile on her face, always willing to lead others in praising God. It was not only recognised within the church, but she was also known as helpful and always smiled as she walked around our village. Even when I visited Liz when she was in hospital, I was always greeted with a wonderful smile.

It is important to be real here. I don't imagine for one minute that Liz always had a smile on her face. She wasn't a superhuman with a permanent smile. I know from the few times we met and shared together how tough our journeys were. And I am fully aware that there will have been times when the smile wasn't there. However, Liz was incredibly consistent in having a smile, being full of joy every time she was seen on walks, came to church, came to a meeting ... the truth is that this was a choice. Again, in the Bible, Christians are often taught to clothe themselves with certain things. For example, in Colossians 3:12 as Christians we are told, "Therefore, as God's chosen people, holy and dearly loved, clothe yourselves with compassion, kindness, humility, gentleness and patience."

Liz made a choice to put on her smile. We all have the choice to put on a smile. Of course, we may not feel like it and may not feel like being kind to someone or being patient in a certain situation. That doesn't mean we can't choose to be kind or patient. I know that every time Liz left her house to go for a walk, she didn't necessarily feel like smiling. But just like a hat or some shoes, Liz chose to put on joy and to put on a smile. This not only had a positive impact on her life, but also on the people she met and even walked past.

There is a beautiful verse in Proverbs 31:25 which states "strength and dignity are her clothing and she smiles at the future". There was something about Liz's faith in God that truly impacted her on the inside and resulted in living a life that oozed strength and dignity; it enabled her to smile despite the circumstances. I believe this was rooted in her deciding to respond to the Bible and rejoice always. Everyone has the choice, or not, to involve God in their lives. It is a choice we make to praise God. Liz was someone who loved to praise. She loved the Psalms which declare: "Praise the Lord, my soul; all my inmost being, praise His holy name." To rejoice and praise God in this way affects your inmost being; it comes from within and therefore overflows out of your life. Liz's praise, joy and smile was a choice that came from deep within her as she dedicated her life to praising God.

Pray continually

The verses in 1 Thessalonians tell Christians to rejoice always and pray continually. Liz was not only an example to me because of her rejoicing, she was also an incredible woman of prayer. This wasn't just something that she did privately, it was quite public. I can remember being caught off guard a couple of times as we would suddenly be praying for someone. This was because prayer to Liz was talking to a friend. It was talking and listening to Jesus. Something that wasn't limited to a church building, a set time in a day when you concentrate on God. It was a way of life, a call on her life, a response to the Word of God, something that these verses tell us to do continuously. There was nothing fake, nothing about being super-spiritual or anything like that. This was real life talking to God like you would eat your breakfast or brush your teeth.

Liz had a desire to see the church pray and would commit to different prayer meetings. Rarely would there be a prayer meeting of any sort, in any church in Linton, without Liz being there. But it wasn't limited to that. I have seen her pray for people in the street, in the park, with nurses. Whenever Liz got the chance to invite others to pray, she would. There was nothing awkward about it. You didn't need to sit down, go into a building or close your eyes. This was real life, involving God in your daily life. Maybe this is why she knew when to text me, when I needed that word of encouragement. This didn't just happen to me. I know of others that seemed to get a text or a call at just the right time from Liz. Why? I would suggest it was because she was in that place of prayer, talking and listening to God. This would have led her to do certain things at certain times as God willed for her life.

Give thanks in all circumstances

Liz was a great example to me of clothing herself with joy and deciding to rejoice. She was also consistent in prayer, always looking at encouraging and involving others in a life of prayer. But there is another thing that the verses in 1 Thessalonians speak of being God's will for us. That is to give thanks in all circumstances. This is tough. How can we give thanks in all circumstances? Again, this, I believe, is a choice. We are not told to give thanks for our circumstances, we are told to give thanks in all circumstances. I often find that a difficult situation is not resolved until I rejoice in God and am thankful that God is with me and is greater than my circumstances. A simple example of this is that I sometimes get extremely tired, even if I have had a good sleep. Sometimes, it is the right thing to do and I can go back to bed. Sometimes, I can't and I find that if I start thanking God for the day, the opportunities the day holds, the strength I have, I gradually feel stronger and breakthrough the tiredness.

I want to share with you the first six verses of Psalm 95: "Come, let us sing to the LORD! Let us shout joyfully to the Rock of our salvation. Let us come to Him with thanksgiving. Let us sing psalms of praise to Him. For the LORD is a great God, a great King above all gods. He holds in His hands the depths of the earth and the mightiest mountains. The sea belongs to Him, for he made it. His hands formed the dry land, too. Come, let us worship and bow down. Let us kneel before the LORD our maker."

This Psalm is a call for Christians to worship God, which Liz loved to do. It is a Psalm that encourages the believer to rejoice because of what God has done. In this case, it is the promise of salvation, which is something that Christians can have utter confidence in if they believe the promises in the Bible to be true. We are to come to God with thanksgiving. We are to sing songs to Him. Notice, it is not to do these things because of what God will do, it is because of who God is: "For the Lord is a great God, a great King above all gods." The earth, mountains, sea and land belong to Him because He made them. So, let us worship Him. If our faith, joy, prayers, praises and thanksgiving were down to what we receive from God, we have a problem straight away. Life is sometimes tough; sometimes things don't go well; sometimes we get ill; sometimes we lose someone; sometimes we are desperate ... that is life! The Psalmist reminds us that we don't worship God for what we get from Him; we do it because of who we know Him to be and for what He has already done.

Understanding this and knowing this in her heart meant that Liz could be thankful in all circumstances. You see, her thankfulness was not because of her situation. It wasn't even just in what she believed God would do for her. Her thankfulness in all circumstances was because she knew God personally, believed His promises and knew what He had already done for her. Maybe this kind of thankfulness gave her more years and less pain. I certainly don't know that, but I imagine that there is truth in it.

Death is not defeat

When Liz passed away and went to glory, I didn't find it easy. As I have described and there is so much more that can be said, Liz was an incredible woman of faith. I believe that the God I worship, in Jesus Christ, is the Healer. There are examples of God healing both in the Old Testament and the New Testament times. I also have seen God heal today. I find it hard to believe that a God who created the world and demonstrated healing power throughout Scripture, couldn't or wouldn't heal today. Furthermore, I believe that—and I appreciate that this may seem crazy to some—everything for everyone's healing need was accomplished when Jesus died and rose from death over two thousand years ago. I will do my best to unpack that last sentence.

The prophet Isaiah tells us of Jesus, "He was pierced for our rebellion, crushed for our sins. He was beaten so we could be whole. He was whipped so we could be healed." The Bible also tells us in the book of Matthew (8:17) "He took our sicknesses and removed our diseases". Clearly, this does not mean that no one ever gets sick or that people don't die from diseases. I am not denying the cancer that I am having treatment for and the cancer that Liz had. But I believe, with complete conviction, that in Jesus there is wholeness and full healing. How that fully works out for me today is a mystery but that doesn't mean it's not a reality. Hebrews 11:1 says, "Faith shows the reality of what we hope for; it is the evidence of things we cannot see." I believe that Jesus removed my diseases on the Cross, I believe this like evidence, proof, confirmation. I am confident in this. I may not fully understand, but I believe it without denying pain and suffering. Even as I write this, there is a sense that some people may well read this thinking, "How can this be? This man sounds crazy."

I look at this like this, if someone was to say, "I believe in God," most people wouldn't see it as an outrageous thing to say. It is quite acceptable, in most cases, for someone to say they have some kind of faith that God exists. Equally, in most cases, especially in our culture, it wouldn't be seen as an outrage if someone were to say, "I do not believe in God." I think it is far crazier to not believe in a God than to believe in a God. Just the reality of creation and life as we know it makes it a certainty to me that there is an existence of a higher force. That higher force for me is the Creator God and can be known personally through Jesus Christ. I believe that from what I understand about the Bible, but also my personal experience of encountering Jesus. Whatever, our reasoning for believing in God, to then either limit God's power, or presume God can't be actively involved in our lives today as He pleases, is quite strange.

My point is that there was a battle in my mind when Liz passed away, simply because I was believing with her and with others that she would be healed. The faith for a miracle was strong. This is a difficult and challenging subject, when God doesn't seem to answer prayers as we imagine them answered. I don't think we can ignore this. But the truth is and I really do not see this as a cop-out for my faith, on the morning that Liz passed she received her complete and total healing.

The evening before Liz passed away, I called a prayer meeting in the church. Many prayed and as we started to pray, a storm started. It was incredible. The rain came down and lightning struck in a way that was very clear and obvious. We stopped the meeting to refer to what was happening. God was not only demonstrating His power but He was letting us know He was there. It was Liz's time. She had served God incredibly well, leading many to look to Him. She was certainly a good and faithful servant of God. Right till the very end, Liz had remained very faithful in her faith.

It was clear that even though Liz did not receive her healing in her mortal body, this wasn't a "lack of faith". My biggest struggle is there was incredible faith and this is where I have to hold my hands up! I don't fully understand the full outworking of how healing takes place in our bodies. I totally believe in a God that has healed and can heal, I know it happens and I still say it has already happened. Sometimes, healing takes form through the supernatural power of God; sometimes God uses people and medication to demonstrate His power. But there is a deeper and profound truth Liz's husband, Steve, said after Liz's passing: "Death is not defeat!"

In the first five verses of Revelation 21, John shares his vision of what happens to believers when they die: "Then I saw 'a new heaven and a new earth' for the first heaven and the first earth had passed away and there was no longer any sea. I saw the Holy City, the new Jerusalem, coming down out of heaven from God, prepared as a bride beautifully dressed for her husband. And I heard a loud voice from the throne saying, 'Look! God's dwelling place is now among the people and He will dwell with them. They will be His people and God Himself will be with them and be their God. He will wipe every tear from their eyes. There will be no more death or mourning or crying or pain, for the old order of things has passed away.'

"He who was seated on the throne said, 'I am making everything new!' Then he said, 'Write this down, for these words are trustworthy and true.'"

This is the victory that Liz now has and it is through Jesus. 1 Corinthians 15:57 says, "But thanks be to God, who gives us the victory through our Lord Jesus Christ." Death is certainly not defeat for Liz and it's not for the many that have faithfully believed and gone before us. It is quite the opposite of defeat, it is victory. Liz is living in the fullness of what God has for her eternally. This is also the victory that we who are left behind have. We have an assurance of faith, that death is not the end but a new beginning to all those who come to Him. We may not yet fully understand but our faith, like Liz's, is in the reality of what we hoped for and the evidence in the things unseen.

I am reminded that when I have reached points of brokenness, that is often the catalyst for a breakthrough from the trial that I am facing.

Chapter Eight
Still Choosing

In chapter two, I wrote about how I had to make daily decisions. It was not just a case of deciding and then running in that direction. In life, we continue to make decisions that determine where we are heading and with what attitude we take with us. For example, the Christian journey of a life of faith is not about deciding one day to follow Jesus and leaving it at that. It involves daily decisions to make good choices regarding our actions, thoughts and motives. Sometimes in my journey of faith, I make mistakes; but it is important that I recognise them as soon as possible and realign myself with how I believe God wants me to live. There are similarities with my journey of living with a diagnosis while having faith that God is my Healer. In my situation, I must continuously make choices that calibrate circumstance to my faith. In this chapter, I will share how this is an ongoing process in my journey.

Prior to my diagnosis, life was pretty good. I was happily married with three wonderful children, good relationships and a job that I loved. Life had its challenges but, generally, things were great. I used to have the standard parent thinking that I didn't want my children to grow up too quickly; I wanted to seize every moment with them. Quite dramatically, once I was diagnosed, that way of thinking was turned on its head and I had a different perspective. I desperately wanted to see the next thing that my children achieved, the next milestone. This caused mixed emotions as I absolutely wanted to enjoy the moment, but I really was conscious of things I would potentially miss. This is a strange thing to explain if you don't experience the thought, "I may not be around to see that."

There was this one occasion when I was sitting in a school show that one of my children was in. It was one where parents and carers were encouraged to attend. My wife was working and could only attend another showing that evening. Because the showing that I was at was during the day, there were many grandparents with their children enjoying the assembly. I had a great seat and could see my daughter clearly and was enjoying the assembly.

Suddenly, out of nowhere, came a thought that I could not get out of my head. As I looked around and saw many grandparents, I thought, "You will never get the chance to do this as a grandparent." It was totally brutal and crippled me on the inside. Talk about happily enjoying a special family moment to have that dashed away and turned into great sadness—just from a thought! Who would understand? I thought, as I sat fighting the tears. This is a very brutal and real experience that I am sure everyone with a terminal diagnosis regularly encounters. It's sudden and vicious. It's a real thought; it's a potential for me; it's probably a highly reality, medical fact, totally understandable process of thinking. However, in that brokenness I also remember some positive thoughts as I continued to try and engage with the show, while avoiding those around me seeing I was in a mess. I think that cancer research is advancing all the time and maybe there will become a treatment that will help cure the type of cancer I have. More significantly, I begin to think of

Bible verses that help me adjust my thinking. This includes 1 Peter 2:24, which says, "He Himself bore our sins in His body on the cross, so that we might die to sins and live for righteousness; by His wounds you have been healed."

I think of Matthew 10:1, it tells me that: "Jesus called His twelve disciples to Him and gave them authority to drive out impure spirits and to heal every disease and sickness."

Both my understanding of the Scriptures and personal experience is that God heals. He instructed His disciples to do the same and God demonstrates His power today. In this instance, sitting in a school play, no one else knows what's going on. But I am moving from a place of desperation to a place of faith and hope as I repeat these words of Scripture over and over in my mind.

Don't Bottle it!

I don't want to give the impression that as soon as I get challenging thoughts or feel down, I instantly respond in a positive way on all occasions. This isn't always the case. There are times when it isn't as straight forward and I am slow in realigning my thinking. When that happens, it is important not to linger in that position for too long. I have broken down, reacted in a negative way to those close to me and made mistakes, etc. The most damaging example of this was that I would sometimes drink alcohol for pain relief. This started prior to my diagnosis, when I had no medication for pain. I thought this helped. In some immediate ways it did, in that it helped numb pain for a period. But this was never a smart choice. It is something I am embarrassed about even though I can understand why anyone would do that in my position.

The problem was that I allowed this to escalate from a pain relief mechanism to an emotional fix when life was tough. It could be a combination of work-related stress. I love my job, but the truth is that, in my experience, Christian ministry can be very draining and leads to high stress levels. I think that one of my strengths in ministry is also a weakness, in that people feel they can share their problems with me. I love that this is something many people feel they can do and I wouldn't want this to change. I also see it as a great privilege and something I am called to do. I wouldn't want people to feel they couldn't speak to me. But I am sharing the realities of the job. It reminds me of the saying, "A problem shared is a problem halved." If there is any truth in it, then the person who is hearing the problem is taking on an element of that problem. The more problems they share in, the more burdens they carry. This is just one example of how pressures can mount up from a work perspective. Holding down a full-time job, bringing up children while living with a terminal illness isn't a straightforward undertaking. The piling up of different pressures inevitably leads to increased stress and friction in the home life. Drink, or any other substance abuse, will never help anyone long-term and usually leads to increased health issues and breakdown of relationships if not addressed.

Friction in relationships can often be caused because of a lack of empathy about what the other person is experiencing. My experience of living with a terminal illness is very much like a roller coaster ride: there are sudden diversions and lots of ups and downs. Apart from my faith (relationship with God), Lucy and my children are my strongest and most valuable support. Because we live together, we share and experience the ride together. But what is hard to understand and easily overlooked, is that, like a roller coaster ride, our experiences can sometimes be very different. One could thoroughly enjoy the experience or get thrills from it, while it could totally terrify the other. My point is not that anyone would get thrills out of a cancer journey, but their experiences, within the family setting, could be a totally different from that of other family members. It is important to remember this with family dynamics, so that patience and understanding can be demonstrated to each other. An example of this is that my feelings of living with cancer can be very different from my wife's feelings and my children's feelings. I could be troubled with the thought of missing a certain milestone that I have always taken for granted, or I could be experiencing physical pain. These are things only I experience. Lucy could be troubled by the thought of having to one day cope on her own, or future financial burdens. These are thoughts only Lucy deals with, whereas my children could be worried about my health and may have fears that they will lose their dad earlier than they would like. Again, these are only thoughts my children will have.

As I said in chapter five, it's good to talk. Good is an understatement: communication is essential in relationships if we are going to understand each other's position. Without question, though, the one thing that we do that helps us overcome family frictions is to pray together. The Bible gives us a great description of how we are to live:

"Therefore if you have any encouragement from being united with Christ, if any comfort from His love, if any common sharing in the Spirit, if any tenderness and compassion, then make my joy complete by being like-minded, having the same love, being one in spirit and of one mind" (Philippians 2:1-2).

Our experience is that we use the principles from Philippians 2:1-2 as a policy: in praying together by "sharing our thoughts, sharing our faith and hope for the future, being inspired by His love, sharing our feelings, focusing on one goal". We emerge from our prayer time together inspired and with a greater love for each other and a desire to move on from any friction. We feel stronger, more supported and more unified in order to take on life's trials in unity.

Whatever the trial we face in life, we tend to look for solutions, or are tempted into doing things we wouldn't normally do in that situation. Whether consciously or not, we look for strategies to help us deal with the situation that we are in. We look for things that will ease the pain, bring us strength, help take our minds off the reality of our situation. These are coping mechanisms. The problem often is that many of these "coping mechanisms" are not at all good for us. Alcohol could be fine in moderation, but when it becomes a solution for physical or emotional pain, it becomes a problem and has the potential to become very damaging.

The words in 2 Peter 1:3-8 have become incredibly useful for me if I am ever tempted to reach for a bottle in times of pain or stress: "His divine power has given us everything we need for a godly life through our knowledge of Him who called us by His own glory and goodness. Through these He has given us His very great and precious promises, so that through them you may participate in the divine nature, having escaped the corruption in the world caused by evil desires.

"For this very reason, make every effort to add to your faith goodness; and to goodness, knowledge; and to knowledge, self-control; and to self-control, perseverance; and to perseverance, godliness; and to godliness, mutual affection; and to mutual affection, love. For if you possess these qualities in increasing measure, they will keep you from being ineffective and unproductive in your knowledge of our Lord Jesus Christ."

This is a mind-blowing truth: because of what Jesus has already accomplished and because His Spirit lives in His followers, His divine power has given us everything we need to live a godly life pleasing to God. We have all we need because a believer's personal relationship with God is such that they live in Christ and Christ lives in them. All this is so that we will know His glory in our lives and we will live a life that glorifies Him.

This truth is not exclusive to some believers, every believer inherits these amazing promises. We have been given these promises so we might participate in the divine nature because His Spirit lives within us. We live in Him and He in us. We participate in the sufferings of Christ, but rejoice in as much as you participate in the sufferings of Christ, so that you may be overjoyed when His glory is revealed (1 Peter 4:13). We participate in the glory of Christ: when Christ, who is your life, appears, then you also will appear with Him in glory (Colossians 3:4). And we also participate in the divine glory of Christ: you, however, are not in the realm of the flesh but are in the realm of the Spirit, if indeed the Spirit of God lives in you. And if anyone does not have the Spirit of Christ, they do not belong to Christ (Romans 8:9). Because we now participate in Christ's divine nature, we must aim to act as Christ would. We must turn from the corruption of the world with its evil desires. If we are believers in Jesus Christ and participators in His nature, then we should be growing more like Christ day by day. We are constantly adding further characteristics of God's life and grace to our own lives.

All this is great news for us when we have various temptations that life throws at us. When I am lured with any kind of temptation, I know that God has already given me all that I need to overcome, make the right choices and press on until I attain to the fullness of Christ. Paul writes: "Not that I have already obtained all this, or have already arrived at my goal, but I press on to take hold of that for which Christ Jesus took hold of me. Brothers and sisters, I do not consider myself yet to have taken hold of it. But one thing I do: Forgetting what is behind and straining toward what is ahead, I press on toward the goal to win the prize for which God has called me heavenward in Christ Jesus" (Philippians 3:12-14).

It is interesting that Paul presses on towards the future without letting his past influence what lies ahead. It is very easy to make the mistake of going back over the past instead of forgetting it. Paul could be equally troubled by his past before he started following Jesus, or proud of the great things he had achieved since following Jesus. But he knew that there was more for him, so he forgot the past and kept his focus on Jesus. It enabled him to continue to receive all he needed for the present and ultimately receive the prize of his heavenly award. I find Paul's example incredibly empowering as I thrive to continue my journey of faith making good decisions that help me reach my goals.

I am reminded of a verse I shared in chapter three while I wrote about Sophie. It says, "The tongue has the power of life and death" (Proverbs 18:21). This is true as I think about the people I chose to put around me, particularly when I am feeling low or in need of some kind of encouragement. I have written a lot about the power of words in this book and I do believe that the spoken word can be very effective. I daily see how words can have a positive or negative impact on my children's lives. When a school friend says something negative about them, you can see how this can hurt their feelings. But it can also influence their confidence and decision-making on things they can and can't do. Equally, when a teacher says something positive, their face lights up, they develop an increase in confidence and feel empowered to go further. Adults are no different: words affect us, sometimes without us even realising. I find that there are some people I speak to and I find their negative words, either about themselves or my situation, leaving me feeling discouraged and disheartened. On the other hand, there are people who speak affirming words of reassurance, hope, faith and health. I always leave these conversations uplifted and wanting to speak to them again soon. Being conscious about putting myself around people who speak positive and affirming words cultivates an atmosphere that I want to foster in my and my family's life.

As I conclude this chapter and consider the ups and downs and the continuous decision-making that are made during the trials that I face in life, I am reminded that when I have reached points of brokenness, that is often the catalyst for a breakthrough from the trial that I am facing. It is true that when someone is in a broken state, they often, at that point, realise their own limitations and look for some kind of solution. For me, Jesus is the answer. I have continuously found that in my seasons of brokenness, Jesus has consistently been there and has been the source of strength that has launched me into a season of strengthening. Psalm 34:18 puts it this way: "The LORD is close to the brokenhearted and saves those who are crushed in spirit."

She explained that when she felt worried about something, she thanked God that she had peace and did not need to be afraid. She repeated it, declaring it over her situation and began to feel at peace.

Chapter Nine

Victory in the valley!

In chapter four, I wrote about the topic of suffering. I looked at Psalm 23 and verse four of that Psalm says, "Even though I walk through the darkest valley, I will fear no evil, for You are with me; Your rod and Your staff, they comfort me."

It is true that we can have victory in the valley. This is the case when we put our trust in Jesus Christ. Victory is not necessarily the absence of trouble, in most cases it isn't. To have victory, you must overcome something. The victory can be attained in the midst of the trouble (valley) by knowing God's presence and comfort right in the middle of your suffering. I want to introduce you to something that I use to help me during times of suffering; it helps me to not only live in victory in the valley but sees me through to the other side of the valley. 'The Faith Wall' is something that has and continues to inspire me towards victory in my life and something my oldest daughter Jessica introduced to me.

Faith Wall

One day, in 2020, when I was three years into my diagnosis, my eleven-year-old daughter, Jessica, took me into her room to show me something. She sat me down on her bed and said, "Look at this." There was a collage of pictures and writings on her wardrobe door. It looked beautiful and well presented. I asked her what it was and she replied, "My Faith Wall". I asked, "What's a Faith Wall?" She explained, "It is a wall full of pictures, drawings, cards, writings and Bible verses."

Basically, my daughter had created a wall in her bedroom that she goes to at different times. She told me that when she had a bad day at school, maybe she struggled in a certain class and didn't fully understand what she was being taught, she would go to her 'Faith Wall' and search for a Bible verse she had highlighted. She came across Philippians 4:13, which states, "I can do all this through Him who gives me strength." She explained that when she felt lacking in strength for something, she found the verse and declared it several times out loud. As she did it, she felt strength rising up inside. She began to feel different about her situation and felt God giving her the strength to overcome.

She continued by saying that when she felt anxious about struggles at home or any situation, she looked for something that gave her hope. She found John 14:27, which says, "Peace I leave with you; My peace I give you. I do not give to you as the world gives. Do not let your hearts be troubled and do not be afraid." She explained that when she felt worried about something, she thanked God that she had peace and did not need to be afraid. She repeated it, declaring it over her situation and began to feel at peace.

When she had a friendship issue or felt as though she was in a situation where it appeared there was no hope, she pointed to a card that stated, "For nothing is impossible with God." (Luke 1:37 ESV) She began to speak out, "I know I feel this situation is impossible, but you say nothing is impossible, I believe it." She explained to me that as she does it, the size of the problem reduced in her mind and she had confidence to approach and resolve the issue.

I was reduced to tears at that point as I saw how effective and wise my daughter had become with practical faith. I was in awe as I looked at her 'Faith Wall' and her explanation about how she used it. I saw a list of random names on the wall and asked who they were. She replied it was a list of people she prayed for. I saw another list of names and asked the same question. She explained they were people who were responding and asking questions about Jesus.

A faith wall is something every Christian should have. It is an incredibly practical way of using the promises that God has for us in our daily lives. We all have moments where we feel excited and good about our circumstances when life is going well and we feel genuinely happy. Equally, we all have times when life is tough, we get bad news, feel disheartened, are unwell, discouraged and, frankly, down. Our response when we have negative feelings are important. When we are low about something, we can feed that feeling. It could be as simple as going over that thought in our minds.

An example could be if I have a particular day when I am discouraged about my illness and start feeling sorry for myself. This is understandable and no one should beat themselves up about such thoughts. But, from my experience, it often leads to other negative thoughts and negative professions over my life. I could begin to think of how my life could end prematurely, or how I could miss certain things in my life like a certain anniversary milestone, or special event in one of my children's life.

There is often a snowball effect that increases my anxiety and fear. It begins to cripple me and influences my emotions and how I live my life. It can also affect those around me, especially those I love. Again, this isn't something people should beat themselves up about, this is natural and understandable. But I have found that we can turn this kind of thinking or mentality on its head and create a more positive outlook. The example of the faith wall does exactly that: it refocuses our thinking. This mentality and mindset enables us to have victory in the valley.

I now have my own 'Faith Wall' in my study that I use daily. I find that it is an incredible tool that helps me be positive, align my thinking, be motivated, thankful for what I have and generally creates a joyful spirit within me. In chapter two, I end with sharing some promises from the Bible that are followed by personal declarations. These are examples of the kind of things I would put on a faith wall.

Preaching from the pit

I am in a privileged position as a church minister. A huge part of my job is to inspire people; to encourage them in faith and to have a positive influence over their life. I am called to serve God and to serve people by sharing the Good News of the Gospel message of Jesus. This includes offering hope, no matter what our circumstances; forgiveness, despite the hurt; peace, no matter what the fear and trouble people are living with; and reconciliation, no matter what pain has been caused. I see preaching as a great responsibly that is not to be taken lightly.

Ultimately, I believe the responsibility of preaching is to bring God's message to His people. What a privilege! What a responsibility! I can be honest that this privilege and responsibility has resulted in a respectful nervousness about preaching; this was especially the case when I started to preach.

Someone who I respect and had a huge influence over my life, once told me: "You know when to stop preaching: it's when you stop being nervous about the responsibility." What they were implying was that once you preach in your own strength, without having the sense of responsibility, you stop. I think this is great advice.

There have been occasions in the last six years where the last thing I feel like doing is stepping up on the platform and speaking blessings and hope. Not because I didn't want to do that, but because I have been searching for those things myself. I didn't feel strong enough, or capable of, bringing God's news to others because I wasn't always in that right place myself.

Although it may not feel like it, this is a positive position for me to be in because I have no choice, unless I feel like quitting my job. So, I must drag myself on occasions to get up and speak truth and God's Word to others; this can have a transforming affect on my own journey. I often feel like the word I speak is just what I need to hear: God is speaking into my life as I hope to speak into other people's life. I don't always find it easy to pick myself up every week to preach, especially when I am having a particular struggle. I also find that I need to protect Saturday evenings, as something will often happen that could potentially disrupt my approach for Sunday. For me, it is vitally important that when I get up to preach, I am in the best possible place with God and with others; therefore, it provides me with a natural discipline that enables me to keep my focus on God.

The Bible tells us to "preach the word; be prepared in season and out of season; correct, rebuke and encourage—with great patience and careful instruction," (2 Timothy 4:2). It tells me that as a church leader, I am to preach God's Word, not my own thoughts or ideas. I must correct, rebuke and encourage others with the patience that comes from sincere love. The only way for me to effectively do this is to remain in unity with God's Spirit and will for my life. So, if I cultivate bad habits, I know it will put a barrier between myself and God. Or if I preach from a place of unforgiveness or anger in my own heart, I am limiting how God may use me. In a sense, the discipline of regular preaching is an incentive to remain in a place of unity with God so that I can be empowered to preach on any occasion and in any season. The incentive is not to preach from a place of disunity with God, but to be aware of attitudes and feelings that can restrict how God uses me.

Ultimately, this means that when I don't feel like preaching or am struggling for inspiration, I do what we saw Paul do in the previous chapter (Philippians 3:12-1): I press on towards my goal; I keep going, I dig deep, I find inspiration, I step out in faith, I persevere. I find that when I do this and share from my place of vulnerability while looking to and trusting in God, it is then when my words seem to be more effective.

We read in Psalm 44:4-8:

4 You are my King and my God, who decrees victories for Jacob. **5** Through you we push back our enemies; through your name we trample our foes. **6** I put no trust in my bow, my sword does not bring me victory; **7** but you give us victory over our enemies, you put our adversaries to shame. **8** In God we make our boast all day long and we will praise your name forever.

This is effectively saying that when we, as followers of God, stop trusting in our own skills, strength and abilities and begin trusting in what God can do through us, He has more freedom to use us as instruments for His purposes. This is not to say that God doesn't use our skills, strengths and natural abilities—of course God uses them; it does, however, help us to get our priorities straight and boast in God, rather than ourselves.

I find that if I make time to visit my faith wall before I get up to preach, it is a practical and positive thing to do. What I am doing is choosing to get right with God, making sure there is no unforgiveness in my heart towards others; making sure I am forgiven by God; making sure I am thankful and inspired by the promises that God gives me, rather than how I feel at one particular moment. Never have I left feeling discouraged after visiting my faith wall, but inspired to ask for forgiveness and speak victorious promises over my life. Every single time I practice this, I am encouraged, motivated and spiritually empowered to face whatever is before me. Of course, this is not limited for use as a preparation for preaching. It becomes a way of life, something that is done whenever I get the opportunity.

What I have found to be a wonderful outcome is that the more I visit my 'Faith Wall', the more I become familiar with God's promises. As I become more familiar with God's promises, my 'Faith Wall' becomes more of a lifestyle that can be accessed from within rather than a place in my house. This does not mean that it becomes ineffective or unused, rather, it is the opposite. My desire is to use it regularly so I become increasingly aware of God's Word and how I can use it continuously throughout each day. My 'Faith Wall' has inspired me and equips me to have victory in the valleys that I face in daily life.

I think this is the highest form of praise – there is nothing better than someone praising God when they are in a mess.

Chapter Ten

Even if?

In this final chapter, I want to share three steps I believe can inspire us to enable us to overcome, receive breakthrough and see God move in power in our situation today. In September 2022, I preached a sermon entitled "Even if?" It was based on a story from the Old Testament book of Daniel. The story is known as the image of gold and the blazing furnace. It is about Babylonian King Nebuchadnezzar, who ascended the throne in 605BC. We join the story in the book of Daniel, chapter 3:

> King Nebuchadnezzar made an image of gold, sixty cubits high and six cubits wide and set it up on the plain of Dura in the province of Babylon. He then summoned the satraps, prefects, governors, advisers, treasurers, judges, magistrates and all the other provincial officials to come to the dedication of the image he had set up. So the satraps, prefects, governors, advisers, treasurers, judges, magistrates and all the other provincial officials assembled for the dedication of the image that King Nebuchadnezzar had set up and they stood before it.

> Then the herald loudly proclaimed, "Nations and peoples of every language, this is what you are commanded to do: As soon as you hear the sound of the horn, flute, zither, lyre, harp, pipe and all kinds of music, you must fall down and worship the image of gold that King Nebuchadnezzar has set up. Whoever

does not fall down and worship will immediately be thrown into a blazing furnace."

Therefore, as soon as they heard the sound of the horn, flute, zither, lyre, harp and all kinds of music, all the nations and peoples of every language fell down and worshipped the image of gold that King Nebuchadnezzar had set up.

At this time some astrologers came forward and denounced the Jews. They said to King Nebuchadnezzar, "May the king live forever! Your Majesty has issued a decree that everyone who hears the sound of the horn, flute, zither, lyre, harp, pipe and all kinds of music must fall down and worship the image of gold and that whoever does not fall down and worship will be thrown into a blazing furnace. But there are some Jews whom you have set over the affairs of the province of Babylon—Shadrach, Meshach and Abednego—who pay no attention to you, Your Majesty. They neither serve your gods nor worship the image of gold you have set up"

Furious with rage, Nebuchadnezzar summoned Shadrach, Meshach and Abednego. So these men were brought before the king and Nebuchadnezzar said to them, "'Is it true, Shadrach, Meshach and Abednego, that you do not serve my gods or worship the image of gold I have set up? Now when you hear the sound of the horn, flute, zither, lyre, harp, pipe and all kinds of music, if you are ready to fall down and worship the image I made, very good. But if you do not worship it, you will be thrown immediately into a blazing furnace.

Then what god will be able to rescue you from my hand?"

Shadrach, Meshach and Abednego replied to him, "King Nebuchadnezzar, we do not need to defend ourselves before you in this matter. If we are thrown into the blazing furnace, the God we serve is able to deliver us from it and He will deliver us from Your Majesty's hand. But even if He does not, we want you to know, Your Majesty, that we will not serve your gods or worship the image of gold you have set up."

Then Nebuchadnezzar was furious with Shadrach, Meshach and Abednego and his attitude toward them changed. He ordered the furnace heated seven times hotter than usual and commanded some of the strongest soldiers in his army to tie up Shadrach, Meshach and Abednego and throw them into the blazing furnace. So these men, wearing their robes, trousers, turbans and other clothes, were bound and thrown into the blazing furnace. **22** The king's command was so urgent and the furnace so hot that the flames of the fire killed the soldiers who took up Shadrach, Meshach and Abednego, **23** and these three men, firmly tied, fell into the blazing furnace.

Then King Nebuchadnezzar leaped to his feet in amazement and asked his advisers, "Weren't there three men that we tied up and threw into the fire?"

They replied, "Certainly, Your Majesty."

He said, "Look! I see four men walking around in the fire, unbound and unharmed and the fourth looks like a son of the gods."

Nebuchadnezzar then approached the opening of the blazing furnace and shouted, "Shadrach, Meshach and Abednego, servants of the Most High God, come out! Come here!"

So Shadrach, Meshach and Abednego came out of the fire and the satraps, prefects, governors and royal advisers crowded around them. They saw that the fire had not harmed their bodies, nor was a hair of their heads singed; their robes were not scorched and there was no smell of fire on them.

Then Nebuchadnezzar said, "Praise be to the God of Shadrach, Meshach and Abednego, who has sent his angel and rescued his servants! They trusted in him and defied the king's command and were willing to give up their lives rather than serve or worship any god except their own God. 29 Therefore I decree that the people of any nation or language who say anything against the God of Shadrach, Meshach and Abednego be cut into pieces and their houses be turned into piles of rubble, for no other god can save in this way."

Then the king promoted Shadrach, Meshach and Abednego in the province of Babylon.

Wow, what an incredible story! What would you do in this situation? King Nebuchadnezzar built a huge gold image, possibly of himself and ordered everyone bow down and worship it. The consequences of not doing so were extreme: death in a blazing furnace. It's quite understandable that everyone obeyed and bowed down to worship the image, all except three Jewish friends of Daniel; Shadrach, Meshach and Abednego.

The three Jews, full of faith, responded in a way that can help us receive our breakthrough, or miracle, today. Their response in verses seventeen and eighteen gives us three steps that are not limited to this event in Babylon. They responded to King Nebuchadnezzar: "If we are thrown into the blazing furnace, the God we serve is able to deliver us from it and He will deliver us from Your Majesty's hand. **18** But even if He does not, we want you to know, Your Majesty, that we will not serve your gods or worship the image of gold you have set up."

Shadrach, Meshach and Abednego acknowledged, that despite death being on their doorstep, their God was firstly:

1. Able to deliver them

If we imagine the situation that Shadrach, Meshach and Abednego found themselves in and also imagine impossible situations that we may have personally experienced or could potentially experience. If alongside that, we have faith in God, a Creator God, that created the heavens and the earth, a God that spoke light into existence and created people in His own image; if we don't think God is able, we have a problem straight away. My faith in God tells me that it isn't too difficult to have the understanding that a Creator God is able to do supernatural things at will.

But it is not always easy to have and demonstrate faith when we encounter challenging circumstances of life.

Whatever challenge we face—it could be a relationship breakdown, a financial issue, a health issue—when that issue is staring us straight in the face as a reality, it isn't always easy to stand in faith.

Shadrach, Meshach and Abednego were facing their issue full on and their earthly king handed them a lifeline and gave them a final chance to bow down and worship the image he had created. This was a bit of a dilemma! Compromise for a moment or get thrown into a furnace. What would you do? I can imagine their friends in the crowd shouting, begging them not to do anything crazy: "Please, just bow down!" "It's not worth it!" "Your God will forgive you..." I love how Shadrach, Meshach and Abednego responded: "If we are thrown into the blazing furnace, the God we serve is able to deliver us from it..."

Wow, what faith in an incredible circumstance! This is bow down or die! We constantly face dilemmas in life; maybe not all like this, but dilemmas where a choice has to be made. To respond in faith is key.

In the New Testament, Jesus healed people on many occasions. I think it's a fair assumption that many more healings were not recorded in scripture. For seven of those recorded healings, Jesus responded "their faith had made them well". To know that God is able is the first step towards personal breakthrough in our own lives. Knowing that God is able is a great starting point but not enough. I don't think it would have been enough to save Shadrach, Meshach and Abednego.

It is one thing to believe that God is able to do anything, but the second step of these three Jews seems to be where the personal faith is considerably stretched. The

Jews confidently declare to King Nebuchadnezzar that their God:

1. Will deliver them

This is a remarkable place to be. The three Jews are on the verge of being thrown into a furnace that is seven times hotter than normal. It is so effective that you don't have to actually get in it for the furnace to kill you. This really is a life-or-death moment, there is no way out. They couldn't run or hide from the situation they were in. Possibly, they could backtrack and bow before and worship the image? But there was something about Shadrach, Meshach and Abednego that caused them to step out with unshakable faith. As the saying goes, they were putting all their eggs in one basket. They were advancing from step one, which was to declare that their God was able to save them from this impossible situation to a declaration in front of the king, all his staff and the whole community, that, "He will deliver us from Your Majesty's hand."

To reach out in faith, knowing that God is able, is one thing, but to say He will deliver us seems to be an advance in faith. Let's remember the situation: bow down or die! Yet they still had the faith to not only believe their God was able to deliver them, but He actually would.

The Bible tells us in 1 Corinthians 15:57: "But thanks be to God! He gives us the victory through our Lord Jesus Christ."

This tells me that as followers of Jesus today, we have more reason to have the same mindset as Shadrach,

Meshach and Abednego. Why? Because we already live in victory through Christ Jesus. This may seem to be a strange mindset for someone who goes through the realities of the trials that life often brings. However, this is a fundamental aspect of the Christian faith: because Jesus Christ was resurrected, we also shall be resurrected; because Jesus attained victory over death, we also shall attain victory over death, forgiveness of sins and eternal life. This is not just a victory for us to obtain when we die and receive eternal life. This is also not just a victory that we obtain when we experience the good things in life. This is a victory that can be obtained in all circumstances and trials that we face each day.

This is not to say we don't suffer, experience emotional or physical pain. Of course we do. But we can have the victory right in the middle of our trial. Notice that Shadrach, Meshach and Abednego didn't miss the furnace. They were tied up and thrown into the blazing furnace. The circumstances or trial of life didn't disappear. Similarly, we aren't exempt from the trials of life. Despite being firmly tied up, they managed to get free and stand tall in the middle of the fire. Their God was with them and they were totally unharmed through their experience. Sometimes our faith can help us stand tall in the middle of our crisis and come out of it unharmed.

We have seen that the three Jews publicly confessed that their God was able to save them. We have also seen that they declared that their God would save them. But there is something else which I believe is incredibly profound in this passage. The final step was that they declared.

2. But even if He does not...

Even if their God does not save them! Even if God does not answer my prayers in the way I imagine! Even if I do not receive full healing! I think there was a time in my Christian journey when I would have thought that was a lack of faith. It was like a "get out of jail card" just in case God doesn't come through. Maybe I wasn't standing firm enough on the promises that I believe God has given us through Scripture? After all, I do believe the prophet Isaiah when he states:

But He was pierced for our transgressions, He was crushed for our iniquities; the punishment that brought us peace was on Him and by His wounds we are healed (Isaiah 53:5).

The words "we are healed" are in the past tense, surely implying that our healing was totally dealt with on the Cross by Jesus Christ over two-thousand years ago. I believe this: that everything for our healing, whatever our prognosis, was overcome by what Jesus accomplished for each one of us when He suffered, died and rose from death. However, it would be strange to believe that suffering no longer takes place. Clearly it does.

I see things quite simply. I have two computers: one is new that I occasionally pick up and use; I also have an older one that is not as good or effective, it can't do the things the newer one can do and certainly isn't as fast or up to date as the newer computer. My problem is I am used to the older one and haven't focused enough to get used to the newer one. Once I get round to becoming familiar with the newer computer, I will become used to it and see the benefits. My point is I own both computers. They are mine and I can use either computer whenever I want. We don't always realise, use or are aware of what we have. I won't realise the benefits of my newer computer until I start using it.

When Shadrach, Meshach and Abednego declared, "Even if He does not," it wasn't a get out of jail free card; it wasn't a backup plan, just in case God didn't or couldn't do something. When we declare in our situation that even if God doesn't, it is not a lack of faith. It is quite the opposite. It is declaring that whatever happens in this life, in our personal situation, we are deciding to trust a God who knows the bigger picture. When we say, "Even if," in our trial, we are putting God at the centre of our situation and putting all our trust in Him. Instead of it being a lack of faith, I think this mentality advances our faith. It is not dependent on what we get from God, but who God is to us and having the faith that God knows best.

I find it interesting that Shadrach, Meshach and Abednego declared God would deliver them before they declared even if He didn't! If we go back to verses sixteen to eighteen from Daniel 3, we see again the three steps in the order they came about: "Shadrach, Meshach and Abednego replied to him, 'King Nebuchadnezzar, we do not need to defend ourselves before you in this matter. 17 If we are thrown into the blazing furnace, the God we serve is able to deliver us from it and He will deliver us from Your Majesty's hand. But even if He does not, we want you to know, Your Majesty, that we will not serve your gods or worship the image of gold you have set up.'"

A danger in the Christian journey is to make it about us rather than Jesus. If you say, "Even if" in a situation, you put God in His rightful place. If our faith is in what God will do for us it would be very vulnerable. Our faith should be in who God is and what He has already done for us. My faith is not conditioned to answered prayers. But the more I praise and the more "even ifs" I declare, the more I see God move in my life. So, Shadrach, Meshach and Abednego were thrown into the incredibly hot furnace and we read:

Then King Nebuchadnezzar leaped to his feet in amazement and asked his advisors, "Weren't there three men that we tied up and threw into the fire?"

They replied, "Certainly, Your Majesty."

He said, "Look! I see four men walking around in the fire, unbound and unharmed and the fourth looks like a son of the gods."

There is no way of knowing this; but would Jesus have turned up if they hadn't declared: "But even if He does not, we want you to know, Your Majesty, that we will not serve your gods or worship the image of gold you have set up." I wonder? Psalm 34:1-3 says:

1 I will praise the LORD at all times. I will constantly speak His praises. 2 I will boast only in the LORD; let all who are helpless take heart. 3 Come, let us tell of the LORD's greatness; let us exalt His name together.

I think this is the highest form of praise – there is nothing better than someone praising God when they are in a mess. When we face any kind of trial we can learn from this incredible account, three simple steps:

1. God is able;

2. God will deliver us;

3. But even if He does not...

That kind of mindset and praise mentality is not a lack of faith, it's a submission to God. When we do this, we place ourselves under the authority of God in our lives. I believe that in that submission, it leads to great blessing and breakthrough. Interestingly, the next verse in Psalm 34 declares: "I prayed to the LORD and He answered me. He freed me from all my fears." David's breakthrough came after the "even if". Praising in the pain leads to breakthrough. When we are at the point of saying, "Even if," we are really saying: "It's nothing to do with me, it's not about me, it's all about Him." Maybe Shadrach, Meshach and Abednego could confidently declare that God would deliver them because they knew that whatever happened, they would worship their God.

CANCER AND THE CROSS

CHRIS KEMSHELL

Conclusion

I can't quite believe I have concluded a book. The sense of personal achievement is quite overwhelming. My hope is that as you have completed this journey with me and that it has been of some help and you feel motivated and somewhat equipped to persevere in your own personal journey, whatever that may involve.

The truth is the topic of healing isn't always a "jukebox" experience, where you put your coin in and get the track you want; in fact, it rarely is. Trusting in God is a lifestyle, it's making decisions to continue to trust and continue to believe, whatever the circumstances you face.

I have no doubt that, as I concluded in the final chapter, the God I serve is certainly able to revive my situation and enable me to experience full healing in this life. Not only do I believe God is able, I believe He will fully heal me. This healing is not down to what God is going to do for me, it is down to me fully understanding what He has already done for me.

Even as I write this, I appreciate that there may be those who simply cannot grasp what I am talking about. The only feasible response I can give is that it is only when we decide to put our trust in God that the mystery of His ways can be remotely understood. I, by no means, have full understanding; I keep pressing on to what I believe is a goal worth pressing on for. This enables me to have the conclusion that "Even If" I don't see the fulfilment of the miracle that my God is able to give me and will indeed give me, I will continue to thank, praise and worship Him all the days of my life. In Jesus Christ, I fully trust and I hope that this book empowers the reader to do the same.

I want to conclude this book by looking at a final piece of Scripture. Hezekiah was an Old Testament king, he was the thirteenth king of Judah and was close to death. We read Isaiah 38:1-8:

In those days Hezekiah became ill and was at the point of death. The prophet Isaiah son of Amoz went to him and said, "This is what the LORD says: Put your house in order, because you are going to die; you will not recover."

Hezekiah turned his face to the wall and prayed to the LORD, "Remember, LORD, how I have walked before you faithfully and with wholehearted devotion and have done what is good in your eyes." And Hezekiah wept bitterly.

Then the word of the LORD came to Isaiah: "Go and tell Hezekiah, 'This is what the LORD, the God of your father David, says: I have heard your prayer and seen your tears; I will add fifteen years to your life. And I will deliver you and this city from the hand of the king of Assyria. I will defend this city.

"'This is the LORD's sign to you that the LORD will do what He has promised: I will make the shadow cast by the sun go back the ten steps it has gone down on the stairway of Ahaz.'" So the sunlight went back the ten steps it had gone down.

Inspired by Jesus's teaching in The Lord's Prayer—which we looked at in chapter four—like Hezekiah, I pray to God and ask Him that He will extend my life so that I see the things I want to see. But even more importantly than that, so I can continue to serve God and inspire others to do the same. But whatever God's plans are for my life and however painful they are, I will always commit to serve and honour Him until I take my last breath.

What Next?

If this book has stirred something up inside of you and you would like to respond in some way, I invite you to start speaking to God. There is not a set format or certain place you need to be to start this conversation. Simply ask God to reveal Himself to you through His Spirit. God loves you and wants to be involved in your life. God is on your side and will help you if you would like to start the journey of relationship with Him.

I encourage you to find a local church and put yourself around people that will encourage you as you start a journey of faith. I also encourage you to get hold of a Bible and start reading it, asking God to speak to you as you read it. You could use this simple prayer as a starting point:

Dear Jesus

I want to start a new life where I put my trust in You. I believe that You died and rose from death for me and want to get to know You. Please come into my heart through Your Spirit and reveal Yourself to me in a personal way. I am sorry for the mistakes I have made and want to spend the rest of my life getting to know You and living for You.

Amen.

Resources

Bible – New International Version (NIV)

The Truth – New Testament study edition by Colin Urquhart

About the Author

Chris Kemshell is the Minister of Linton Free Church, which is a United Reformed Church in South Cambridge, England. Originally from Yorkshire, Chris is a passionate leader whose heart is to see the local church become increasingly relevant in their community. Chris has a wealth of experience in working alongside people in a variety of settings and is driven by a desire to see people enter and develop personal relationship with Jesus Christ.

Ultimately, Chris thrives from seeing people experience the love and power of Jesus for themselves. Chris engages well with people, using humour and drawing on day-to-day circumstances, connecting them to a life of faith.

Chris is married to Lucy and they have three children: Jessica, Luke and Sophie.

CHRIS KEMSHELL

About PublishU

PublishU is transforming the world of publishing.

PublishU has developed a new and unique approach to publishing books, offering a three-step guided journey to becoming a globally published author!

We enable hundreds of people a year to write their book within 100-days, publish their book in 100-days and launch their book over 100-days to impact tens of thousands of people worldwide.

The journey is transformative, one author said,

"I never thought I would be able to write a book, let alone in 100 days... now I'm asking myself what else have I told myself that can't be done that actually can?'"

To find out more visit
www.PublishU.com

Printed in Great Britain
by Amazon

34863479R00089